Liquid Millionaire

How to Make Millions from the Up and Coming Stock Market Boom

by

Stephen Sutherland

authorHOUSE®

AuthorHouse™ UK Ltd.
500 Avebury Boulevard
Central Milton Keynes, MK9 2BE
www.authorhouse.co.uk
Phone: 08001974150

First published by AuthorHouse 1/20/2009

ISBN: 978-1-4389-0328-6 (sc)
ISBN: 978-1-4389-0329-3 (hc)

Printed in the United States of America
Bloomington, Indiana

This book is printed on acid-free paper.

The following disclaimer applies to the extract from Jim Rohn's book, *The Five Major Pieces to the Life Puzzle,* on page 177 of this book:

This content is reprinted from *The Five Major Pieces to the Life Puzzle* by Jim Rohn with permission from Success Media and Jim Rohn International. Opinions expressed by authors are not necessarily those held by Success Media.

READERS ARE RAVING

QUESTION: What do these people have in common?

- ◆ A bestselling author worth £130 million pounds

- ◆ A man who manages a £550 million pound pension fund

- ◆ A multi-millionaire trader and coach

- ◆ A one time world professional futures champion

- ◆ A world leading nanotech investing expert

- ◆ A man who has coached Olympic champions and astronauts

…and bestselling authors, leading authorities in their respected fields, captains of industries, chief executive officers, high-profile executives, pioneers, entrepreneurs and highly respected professionals.

ANSWER: They all love *Liquid Millionaire*.

See for yourself…

"BESTSELLING AUTHOR WORTH £130 MILLION SAYS AUTHOR'S STOCK MARKET BOOM PREDICTION COULD BE RIGHT"

"Inspiring and exciting, and just possibly right."

– **Richard Koch, member of the *Sunday Times* Rich List and author of The *80/20 Principle*, which has sold more than 700,000 copies and been translated into 25 languages. His latest book is *The Star Principle*, sub-titled *How It Can Make You Rich***

"A WINNING SYSTEM, SAYS WORLD LEADING AUTHORITY ON THE DEVELOPMENT OF HUMAN POTENTIAL"

"A winning system."

– **Brian Tracy, author of countless bestsellers including *Million Dollar Habits* and *Getting Rich Your Own Way***

"COACH OF OLYMPIC CHAMPIONS, ASTRONAUTS AND FORTUNE 500 TOP EXECUTIVES PLANS TO BUILD TIME MACHINE AFTER READING *LIQUID MILLIONAIRE*"

"Though it's never too late, I would have loved to study this book much earlier in my investing cycle. Not only will you learn about gaining material wealth, Stephen's advice is full of solid concepts for achieving "inner wealth" as well, dealing with "quality of life" as well as "standard of living.""

– **Dr. Denis Waitley, bestselling author, *The Psychology of Winning***

"ONE TIME WORLD PROFESSIONAL FUTURES TRADING CHAMPION GIVES BIG THUMBS UP TO *LIQUID MILLIONAIRE*"

"Superbly written by the pioneer of ISA Trend Investing, I highly recommend this book."

- **Mark Shipman, Professional Investor and author of *The Next Big Investment Boom* and *Big Money, Little Effort***

"HOW TO CONSISTENTLY MAKE STOCK MARKET PROFITS"

"Stephen Sutherland has identified one of very few ways to consistently make stock market profits in Bull Markets!"

– **Darrell Brookstein, author of *Nanotech Fortunes*; the premier book on successful investing in nanotechnology** www.Nanotechnology.com

"WORLD'S #1 BUSINESS COACH LOVES CHAPTER ON HOW TO READ THE MARKET LIKE A PRO"

"Just the pages on price and volume make it worth reading the entire book. A simple system to get your money working for you ..."

– Bradley J. Sugars, world-renowned entrepreneur, bestselling author, and business coach

"AUTHOR OF OVER 70 BOOKS RECOMMENDS READING *LIQUID MILLIONAIRE*"

"A smart, sensible book on both investing and success. Recommended."

– Robert W. Bly, author of over 70 books including *Persuasive Presentations for Business* (Entrepreneur Press)

"WORLD-RENOWNED AUTHOR AND SPEAKER SAYS TO WIN FINANCIALLY, IT'S ALL ABOUT A SYSTEM"

"Few things affect every area of our life more than our finances. Those who have succeeded financially have always been people with a system. In *Liquid Millionaire*, Stephen Sutherland presents us all with a system so we can begin to learn, grow, and win financially."

– Jim Stovall, author of *The Ultimate Gift*

"BUY WHAT'S RISING, SAYS BESTSELLING AUTHOR"

"Let's see, buy what's falling or buy what's rising? Hmm, choices, choices. I'll go with rising - and so will you after reading this book."

– Jason Kelly, bestselling author, *The Neatest Little Guide to Stock Market Investing*

"A SYSTEM FOR GREAT INVESTING RETURNS"

"A fascinating work that combines important elements of self-development and the prosperity mindset, with an intriguing system for great investing returns."

– Tom Butler-Bowdon, bestselling author of *50 Prosperity Classics* and *50 Success Classics*
www.Butler-Bowdon.com

"ISA TREND INVESTING IS THE FUTURE"

"The ISA Trend Investing Era Cometh."

– Al & Laura Ries, bestselling authors of *The 22 Immutable Laws of Branding* and *The Fall of Advertising & the Rise of PR*

"SURE-FIRE SYSTEM I PLAN ON STARTING NOW"

"Very inspiring and insightful. This is a surefire system I plan on implementing immediately."

– Jack Hodge, CEO of Brain Bender Games and author of *The Power of Habit* and *Grit*

"MULTI-MILLIONAIRE TOTALLY CONVINCED"

"My advice to you all out there is "READ *LIQUID MILLIONAIRE* NOW"!"

– Greg Secker, Multi-Millionaire Trader and Trader Coach
www.tradersuniversity.co.uk

"IT'S A MASTERPIECE"

"Without doubt the most powerful and inspiring book you will ever read. It's a MASTERPIECE!"

– Rob McNinch, Senior Consultant and Head of Operations, ISACO Ltd

"CHAIR OF TRUSTEES WHO MANAGES £550 MILLION PENSION FUND CALLS *LIQUID MILLIONAIRE* OUSTANDING"

"*Liquid Millionaire* is the plain man's guide to building personal wealth through ISA and SIPP investing. It is a refreshing and highly enjoyable read; both educational and stimulating (and should be on your recommended reading list for personal investing). It deserves a 'Plain English - Crystal Award', it is simply outstanding."

– Stephen Swinbank - Professional Investor & Chair of Trustees, NCR Ltd Pension Fund

"TOP MD CALLS IT A NEW WAY OF CREATING WEALTH"

"Stephen Sutherland is ahead of his time in terms of developing a new way of creating financial wealth for people. His caring / value creating attitude in helping his clients is exceptional."

– Nigel Fletcher - Managing Director, Fairfield Displays and Lighting Ltd

"PROPERTY DEVELOPER SCORES *LIQUID MILLIONAIRE* A PERFECT 10 – CALLS AUTHOR A MASTER"

"A seemingly complex subject interestingly explained. Straightforward and openly candid. Would recommend. 10 out of 10 for valuable content, likeability of author, credibility, preparedness of author, overall professionalism of book, integrity / transparency of author. 10 out of 10 overall. Stephen Sutherland is clearly a master of his subject."

– Chris Sturdy - Property Developer and Owner of Sturdy Co Real Estate

"STRONGLY RECOMMENDED READ"

"An excellent and thoroughly recommended read for anyone wishing to take control of their lives and take a big step towards financial independence."

– Paul Moone - Commercial Analyst at Rexam PLC

"A WAY TO GUARANTEE A BRIGHT FUTURE"

"Stephen's latest book *Liquid Millionaire* is so full of hope, you cannot help feel more optimistic about the future. ISACO's *Daily Market Update* has kept me steady in the current market turmoil and I look forward to Stephen's predictions unfolding."

– Clive Nayler - Company Director at Lion Associates Ltd

"DOCTOR AND CLIENT OF AUTHOR SAYS IT'S AN EASY, TIME FRIENDLY, STRESS FREE WAY TO MAKE MONEY"

"For some time I'd been looking for a trustworthy method for making investment decisions that is stress-free and doesn't take up my time. The system offered in Stephen's book meets my criteria - even better, I know his money is invested in the same funds as mine."

– John Tanqueray - G.P. and Company Director of Mulberry House Clinic

"A BRILLIANT CONCEPT"

"*Liquid Millionaire* is an inspirational, no-nonsense guide that is helping me move ever closer towards financial freedom. The concept is brilliant yet, at the same time, it is really easy to understand. I highly recommend this wonderful book."

– Rob Sheil - Managing Director of RS Testing & QA Ltd

"SUCCESSFUL BUSINESS OWNER CALLS *LIQUID MILLIONAIRE* A RAY OF FINANCIAL SUNSHINE"

"Clear, concise and conclusive – a ray of financial sunshine."

– Joe Hellak - Owner of AJH Designs Ltd

"A SIMPLE, SOLID SOLUTION TO LONG-TERM WEALTH"

"If you want a simple, solid solution to long term-wealth, you MUST READ *Liquid Millionaire*. What an investment opportunity! I feel privileged to be a client of Stephen's and when asked to describe him, I always say that he's a straight talking guy who enjoys life, and helping others. I can say that hand on heart, Stephen's system works."

– Steve Jackson - Engineer for Instrument & Control TA and Property Investor

"SHIVERS OF EXCITEMENT DOWN THE SPINE"

"Shivers of excitement down the spine for what is possible in the future."

– John Pearsall - Control Engineer for TRW Electronics

"PHYSIOTHERAPIST CALLS *LIQUID MILLIONAIRE* A MUST READ"

"A must read for anyone who wants to gain control of their financial future and create Tax-Free Wealth. Stephen's book clearly explains his proven system for ISA Trend Investing, which could help you to seriously profit from a potential stock market boom."

– Dominic Bannister - Occupational Health Physiotherapist for Managed Medical Care Ltd

"BUSINESSMAN DEVOURS *LIQUID MILLIONAIRE* IN ONE SITTING"

"I stumbled upon this book and read it all in one go! In *Liquid Millionaire*, Stephen Sutherland shows you easy, time friendly ways to increase your earning ability, safe ways to save your money and most importantly, ways to invest and compound your money into large tax-free amounts."

– Declan Hughes - Owner of Gormley Footwear
www.kidskickers.co.uk

"BUSINESS OWNER SAYS THE READING OF *LIQUID MILLIONAIRE* IS A MUST FOR EVERY INVESTOR"

"A real eye opener, a must for any investor. A valuable tool to have in your investment armoury."

- Richard Neale, Proprietor of R &G Building Services

CONTENTS

This book is dedicated to the best person I have known my entire life, Paul Sutherland, an outstanding individual who is constantly striving to improve himself and the lives of others.

And he's not only my brother but my best friend, weight training buddy and business partner. Paul, I feel truly privileged to be right by your side on this extremely exciting journey.

You're a great guy. Love you, man.

Stephen (left) and Paul Sutherland
Photograph courtesy of Matthew Seed

ACKNOWLEDGMENTS

On the investing side, I'd like to send a huge thank you to Mr William O'Neil who has made all of this possible. I could never have achieved my investing results without him.

Bill, when you wrote in my workbook, "You can do it!" you would not believe how much that meant to me. Thank you for introducing me to some of the greatest investment minds on the planet.

I'd like to show my appreciation to all the people who have taught me the rules, lessons, tips and techniques for successful investing - Bernard Baruch, Gerald Loeb, Jesse Livermore, Nicolas Darvas, Peter Lynch, Jack Schwager, Edwin Lefèvre, Stan Weinstein, Michael Steinhardt, Martin Zwieig, John Train, Oliver Velez, Thomas Meyers, Martin Schwartz, Lois Peltz, Dr R. Bryan Stoker, Dr Alexander Elder, Carl Gyllenram, Van K. Tharp, John Boik, John C. Bogle, Victor Sperandeo, David Saito-Chung, Richard Farleigh, Mark Shipman, Dan Denning, Dr Thomas K. Carr, Curtis Faith, Ari Kiev, Tom McCarthy, Simon Zutshi, Wendy Patton and Justin Ryan.

I'd also like to thank Results Corporation Ltd; the company that introduced me to the "modelling" theory. And in 1998, Results recommended I read Tony Robbins' classic *Awaken the Giant Within*—which proved to be the starting point in helping take my life to a whole new level. Cheers guys. That leads on very nicely to personally thanking Anthony Robbins for the wealth of insights he has bestowed upon me.

And if it hadn't been for Chris Manning, I might never have heard of Bill O'Neil. Chris, you're a hero.

A big thank you also goes to the British Government (past and present) for introducing PEP's in 1987. To the Conservatives for introducing them and to the Labour party for keeping them, I salute you.

I'd also like to thank Brian Tracy; the one personal development author and speaker who has made the biggest positive impact in my life. Brian, you are so inspirational, as well as being extremely intelligent and very generous. Your kind acts have meant the world to both me and my brother Paul. You're an incredible human being.

And I have to say cheers to my friend Jason Dunks for introducing me to Brian back in the late nineties. Thanks Jason for passing on Brian's wonderful audio program; *The Luck Factor*.

My thanks also go to Robin Sharma for introducing me to the power of daily habits and William Glasser who taught me absolute gems such as how to develop mental strength and how to create better relationships—using his groundbreaking choice theory.

I also acknowledge and thank Michael Masterson for helping me understand the power of financially valued skills.

I'd like to thank every single author, speaker, motivator and expert out there who has played their part in instilling their words of wisdom upon me—helping me to act more effectively which in turn has helped me to feel better and get better results - Sir Richard Branson, Sir Tom Hunter, Howard Schultz, Napoleon Hill, Jim Rohn, George S. Clason, Robert Kiyosaki, Charles Albert Poissant, Christian Godefroy, Mark Victor Hansen, Robert Allen, Steve K. Scott, Richard Carlson, Stephen Covey, Ken Blanchard, Spencer Johnson, Michael Gerber, Joe Vitale, Dan Kennedy, Richard Koch, Bradley J. Sugars, Carl Sewell, Seth Godin, Heinz Goldman, Jeffrey Gitomer, Og Mandino, Al Ries and Laura Ries, Jack Trout, Robert Cialdini, Robert Bly, Frank Bettger, Zig Ziglar, Richard Denny, Joe Girard, Neil Rackham, Lester Wunderman, Jay Conrad Levinson, David Andrusia, Rick Haskins, Harry Beckwith, David Garfunkel, Joseph Sugarman, Chet Holmes, Jay Abraham, Drayton Bird, Ted Nicholas, Robert Collier, Dan Poynter, Dale Carnegie, David Schwartz, Susan Jeffers, The Dalai Lama, Hyrum W.

Smith, Wayne Dyer, Jack Canfield, Les Hewitt, Tom Butler-Bowdon, Charlie "Tremendous" Jones, Kevin Trudeau, Peter Post, Wally Amos, Stu Glauberman, Mitch Albom, Earl Nightingale, W. Clement Stone, Daniel Goleman, Sue Wiggins, Nick Williams, Simon Woodroffe, Richard Carlson, Neil Crofts, John C. Maxwell, Maxwell Maltz, Martin Seligman, Les Giblin, Denis Waitley, Matthew McKay, Patrick Fanning, Claude M. Bristol, Nathaniel Branden, Dr David Burns, Albert Bandura, Robert Collier, Robert Ringer, Joseph Murphy, Dr Paul G. Stoltz, Bill Phillips, Kerry and Jan Kay, John Hodgson, Phillip Day, Dr Michael Colgan, Owen McKibbin, Dr Linda Papadopoulos, Ray Kurzweil, Terry Grossman, John Gray, Barbara De Angelis, Dr Neil Clark Warren, Tony Clink, Neale Donald, Muhammad Ali, Hana Yasmeen, Eckhart Tolle, Yehuda Berg, Anthony de Mello, Stephan Bodian, Sylvia Browne, M. Scott Peck, Richard Maurice Bucke, Pitirim A. Sorokin, Gregg Braden, Henry Dreher, Dr James E. Loehr, Peter J. McLaughlin, Scott Bedbury, Viktor E. Frankl, Tony Schwartz, Jack Groppel, Peter Thompson, Larry King, Sir John Templeton, Joe Polish, Dominic O'Brien, Roger Dawson, Harvey Mackay, Darrell Brookstein, Felix Denis, Peter Bielagus, Marc Allen, Mike Litman, Jason Oman, Jim Slater, David Chiltern, Mike Southon, Chris West, John Caples, Sanaya Roman, Jim Stovall, Richard Wiseman, Iain Abernethy, David Myers, Professor Graham Jones, Adrian Moorhouse, Rick Warren, Wallace D. Wattles, Steve Weber, David Meerman Scott, Jim Cathcart, Jack Hodge, Bob Burg, John David Mann, Allen Elkin, Murray Smith, Jason Kelly, Regis McKenna, Bob Proctor, John Assaraf, Lisa Nichols, Michael Beckwith and Sir Alan Sugar.

I've also had (and still have) numerous personal growth influences in my life which have helped play a special part in my development. My thanks go to Nightingale Conant for providing countless cutting edge audio programs, John Thompson, John Bates, Justin Bell, Niri and Catherine Patel, and all the rest of the gang I've met and had fun with at YES Group North.

I'd also like to pay special thanks to our business team—their ability to deliver such an outstanding service to our clients never ceases to amaze me. This includes Rob McNinch—who is the best team member we've ever had the privilege of working with. Rob you're a genius. Plus Steve Todd who I have to say is one of the most reliable people I know–anything that needs doing is never a problem, Mike Davies, our latest high flying recruit, Catherine Madock, our superb accountant, plus all the premium clients who have helped out on a purely voluntary basis at the Tax-Free Millionaire live events. These include Glenn Warhurst, Jon Marshall, John Bristow, Jag Patel, Joe Hellak, Steven Jackson, Chris Nash, Sam Beatson, Thai Bridgen, Paul Bates, Rizwan Kayani, Sarah Readings, Sue Sayers and Lee Anderton.

I'd also like to express my gratitude to our key suppliers and joint venture partners who include our close friends Mark and Virginia Sawyer (The Property Association), plus Nick Laight and "Charlie Wright" (Canonbury Publishing), Greg Secker (Knowledge to Action), Fleet Street Publishing, Chris Howard (Christopher Howard Events), Bob Brown (BizzOpps4U), Damian Qualter (BuyProperty 4Less), Frazer Furnhead (Alchemy Business Development), Andy Shaw (www.andyshaw.com), Every Investor, CLB Accountants, Jason Peake, Kevin Deighton and Matt Bradley (AIS), Tim at EasiPrint, Chris Clark from Clark Marketing Ltd, MoneyPenny, Paul Flintoft, Plum Communications, GP Gem Communications, WebEx, WorldPay, WRG Creative Communication Ltd, United Business Centres plc plus all the team at CRM System Support Ltd.

I'd also like to thank every single person who is, or has been a client of ours. A huge thank you goes to all of the people who kindly volunteered to review the draft copies of this book. And an even bigger one for the people who actually read my manuscript, liked it, and then put pen to paper; you are my heroes! Your thoughts, insights and comments were priceless. I'd also like to say "thank you" to all the people who acted as a go between in helping me to get *Liquid Millionaire* reviewed. You really were so patient, so helpful and so supportive all the way through the process. Also to Victor Risling, president of Brian Tracy International, thanks once again Victor for helping us out.

I'd also like to say how grateful I am to all the people who have helped in some way to make and maintain our "quality" world - Trisha Neild and Karen Harrop (ladies, you are Super Fantastic!), the whole crew at Ashton Chiropractic Clinic, including Anne, Steve, Lisa and Lynley

- Phillip & Jane Noble and their team at Noble Dental Practice, the team at Esporta, John Walton the magnificent car detailer (and martial arts master), Leslie Dean my superb hairdresser, Nick the podiatrist, the fabulous team at the Lowry Hotel in Manchester, including Marc Whitley, Marco, Sherman (Cool Runnings), Jonathan, Irfan, Bavand, Marianne, Stella, Matthew, Oliver Thomas (Head Chef), Keith, Andy, Peter, Michael and Pino - Graham our very reliable taxi driver, Carol at Johnsons the dry cleaners, Dave and his crew who do a great job maintaining our gardens, David, Karim and Fiona, from Armani Collezioni in Manchester, LifeFitness, Amazon.co.uk, Nike, Morningstar, Ameritrade, E*Trade, CNN, Profunds, Microsoft, Intel, Medved, Nescafe and Tesco.

I must also say thank you to all the people involved in creating this book and making a dream become a reality - Daniel Cooke, Elaine Sinfield, Bob de Groff, Jessica Sheese, Blake Muntzinger and the rest of the fabulous team at Authorhouse, Siobhan Curham (Siobhan, you are a real delight to work with), Mindy Gibbins-Klein, Jenna Gould, Amy Larman, Tina McKenzie, Stuart Berry, Avril Ehrlich, Charlie Hankers, George Foster, Al Taylor, Pannone and Partners, Matthew Seed, Yahoo, Getty Images, Morningstar, William O'Neil + Companies Inc, Nationwide Building Society, Financial Express, IStockPhoto.com and Digital Turtle.

On the personal side, I'd like to thank Mum and Dad for their continued unconditional love and support. Mum, Dad, your words of encouragement always give Paul and me a serious lift. I am so thankful to you for all you've done and continue to do.

Huge thanks go to you, Paul who I'm so grateful to for all the love, the laughs, the help and support that help make my life so incredibly rewarding.

And to you the reader for buying this book, I'm truly grateful and hope that you get as much from reading it as I got from writing it.

Finally, just in case I forgot to mention you, I want to thank all the people that I mistakenly forgot to acknowledge. I really did think that I'd covered all bases but if I did slip up, I apologise.

"Follow the Trend–The Trend Is Your Friend."

– Jesse Livermore
Legendary Stock Market Investor

BONUS

3 FREE Special Wealth Building Reports (RRP: £497)

Special Report 1 How to Help Your Children Retire at Age 45 with a £9.2 Million Pound Fortune

Special Report 2 How to Increase Your Income x 10 over the Next 3 ½ Years

Special Report 3 A Secret Skill That Few People Know That Could Help You Easily Earn over £1 Million Pounds per Year

Download Your £497 of FREE Goodies Today at:

www.ISACO.co.uk/content/book

But why give close to £500 worth of product away for free? What's the catch?

There is no catch. The reason I decided to do this is because if you like the information found in the special reports, you may end up one day becoming a client. Of course, the information is not going to appeal to everybody but you just might be one of those people who love it. And if you came on board, and joined our club, that would be a win for both you and me.

A NOTE TO THE READER FROM PAUL SUTHERLAND

Former British Prime Minister Benjamin Disraeli said, *"The secret of success in life is for a man to be ready for his opportunity when it comes."*

Get yourself ready, because what you are about to learn could be the investment opportunity of a lifetime!

I would be very surprised if you weren't grabbed by the information presented to you in this book...but then again it is not suited for everybody. Would learning how it might be possible to make millions from an up and coming stock market boom interest you?

Good, because like my brother Stephen, I also believe that over the next 10-20 years, we are probably going to see the stock market explode—and soon you are going to see plenty of evidence to back up this prediction. Let me give you a quick example.

If you are familiar with charts, you will be able to clearly see (from the image below) what is known as a "cup-with-handle" formation.

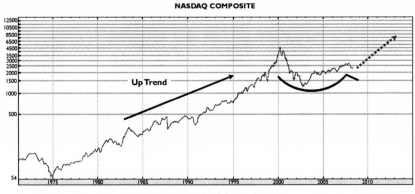

Data Supplied by Yahoo.

This image is the long-term chart of the Nasdaq Composite (US Technology Index). The pattern "cup-with-handle" is named as such because it resembles the outline of a coffee cup with a handle. Stocks, funds, sectors, industry groups and indexes can all form this very positive pattern. It is well known amongst technical investors and "chartists" as one of the most bullish and dependable chart patterns around. And many a big upside move has been made off such a pattern.

And so when you see a major index such as the Nasdaq create such a formation, especially over a long period of time, it's time to get excited. As you will later discover, sometimes, stocks, funds, sectors and indexes can get ahead of themselves. When they do this (as the Nasdaq did with the tech bubble in the late nineties and early 2000) they have got to correct in price—before *eventually* moving back into higher ground. This is both normal and natural.

From looking at this chart pattern, the Nasdaq is therefore indicating that it might be setting up for a big move to the upside. This would make a lot of sense. After all, the Nasdaq is the US technology index and you'd have to have been living in a cave not to notice that right now we are in the middle of a global information revolution.

And what is exciting about this is that the Nasdaq is still trading way below the price where it topped out in March 2000.[1] The Nasdaq has made no progress since 2000… but technology certainly has. And that tells you that sooner or later, the Nasdaq is going to have to play catch up. Let me explain by giving you some facts and figures.

Let's talk first about the internet. I am sure that you will agree the internet seems to sit at the core of the information revolution. According to the UK Statistics Authority, in Great Britain there are approximately 24.4 million households. In 1999, the year before the stock market topped out, 16.3% of these 24.4 million had access to the internet.

But in 2007, 61% of UK households had internet access.[2] That's a 282% increase in just 8 years. So when people say that the technology boom has been and gone, they do not know what they are talking about. For example, did you know that only 1 billion (15.2%) of the world's estimated 6.6 billion people are currently online?[3] And at the moment only a tiny 4.5% of the worldwide population are accessing the internet using fast broadband connections.[4]

You don't need to have an IQ of 170 to realise that there is still plenty of room for growth. Mobile phone subscriptions worldwide have also seen 200% growth since 2001. In 2001, there were just under 1 billion mobile phones in use, but in 2008, that number had ballooned into more than 3 billion.[5] Plus new developments in biotechnology and nanotechnology could also help the stock market surge over the next decade or two.

In his book, *Nanotech Fortunes*, author Darrell Brookstein stated:

"Beginning some time between 2006 and 2008 the U.S. (and other securities markets worldwide) will experience the first of many nanotech stock booms that will occur periodically for decades—at least until sometime between 2025 and 2050."

Keeping with the technology theme, in the excellent book, *Fantastic Voyage* (of which you will be hearing more later), you learn that co-author Ray Kurzweil spent several decades studying and modelling technology trends and the impact they had on society. Here is just a snippet of what Kurzweil and co-author Terry Grossman had to say about the future:

"...the rate of change is itself accelerating. This means that the past is not a reliable guide to the future UNLESS WE TAKE THE ACCELERATION INTO ACCOUNT. The 20th century was not 100 years of progress at today's rate but, rather, was equivalent to about 20 years, because we've been speeding up to current rates of change.

And we'll make another 20 years of progress at today's rate, equivalent to that of the entire 20th century by 2014. And then we'll do it again in just 7 years. Because of this exponential growth, the 21st century will equal 20,000 years of progress at today's rate of progress–1,000 times greater than what we witnessed in the 20th century, which in itself was no slouch for change.

The result will be profound changes in our lives, from our health and longevity to our economy and society, even our concepts of who we are and what it means to be human."

Ray goes on to say:

"As we peer even further into the 21st century, nanotechnology will enable us to rebuild and extend our bodies and brains and create virtually any product from mere information, resulting in remarkable gains in prosperity."

If that does not inspire you, then you may need to check your pulse. The thing is, I am pretty sure you will agree, the world *is* and *has* been changing at a rapid pace. And this high-speed advancement in technology could possibly create a stock market boom, especially with the market not making any price progress for almost a decade. But let's put the advancement of technology to one side for a moment because I am guessing that what you *really* want to know is:

~ Does this new system of investing, that Stephen is about to share with you, really work?

~ Will it be able to help you to capitalise on what could be a major move in the stock market?

The answer to both questions is–yes, absolutely.

When you know what you are doing, or if you have the right help and support, it's really easy to find the "best of the best" investment vehicles to park your money into.

But because three out of four investment funds always move in the direction of the market,[6] you do need to get in sync with the market's trend (direction) or you will lose money nearly every time. <u>The real key then is knowing how to read the *trend* of the market</u> and I promise you that Stephen is going to show you exactly how to do that—and after he is finished, you will be reading the market just like the pros.

So when you combine reading the market direction with finding the right investment funds, you simply wrap an ISA (Individual Savings Account) or SIPP (Self Invested Personal Pension) around your investment and you've cracked it. In other words, when you put all the pieces of the puzzle together, it really is possible to make some serious tax-free money. For example, the investment fund search tool (HIRE CAR™) that Stephen personally created, managed to find the Number 1 fund in 2003, which made a gain of 91.05%.[7] And yes, we did invest all our ISA money into it.

Was picking the Number 1 fund of 2003 simply down to good luck?

Well, I will let you be the judge of that, because in the following year, 2004, the ISA Trend Investing System that Stephen created beat the Nasdaq fourfold and in 2005 it beat the Nasdaq tenfold.[8]

Whenever Stephen and I reminisce about one of the funds that his system found; one that we and our clients bought, it always brings a smile to our face. It was called the Legg Mason Japan Fund and when it moved it really did take off like a rocket. In just 12 weeks, it jumped 49.7%.[9]

Plus…. yes, there is more!

Stephen's system went on to help us and our clients find AND invest in the Number 1 and the Number 3 top performing funds over the 2003-2007 bull market.[10]

The Number 1 performing fund of the 03-07 bull market is called the Invesco Perpetual Latin America Fund. It gained 587.8%, beating the Nasdaq by almost six times and averaging 47% per year over that 5 year period.[11]

The Number 3 performing fund of the 03-07 bull market is called the Scottish Widows Latin America Fund. This one gained 492.3%, beating the Nasdaq by almost five times and averaging 42.7% per year over that 5 year period.[12]

When people ask me does it work, I tell them that this unique way of investing using ISAs and SIPPs has so far helped Stephen and me to build up six figure, tax-free accounts. But sometimes the best way to answer that question is through the mouths of our clients.

Our clients are mostly high net worth individuals and come from various backgrounds. You will discover more about them later in the book. I personally think the best people to ask are the people who not only use the system but ones who have been with us the longest. In other words, clients who have seen how the system works through a full stock market cycle (a bull (up) market and a bear (down) market). In case you are wondering, a full cycle tends to last for about 5 years.[13]

Stephen recently spoke to three of these long serving clients and they had this to say.

"I have complete confidence in the system." John Bristow.

Client, Jon Marshall was ecstatic about "being in cash" when the recent bear market struck and the Nasdaq plunged a horrible 24.7%.[14] His exact words were, *"It's a good job the system told us to get out onto the sidelines. If we wouldn't have got out of the market, I would have lost a lot of money."*

"I have 100% faith in the system." Glenn Warhurst.

And even more recently, just after we got back into the market,[15] Glenn sent Stephen a personal email.

Here's what it said:

Subject Heading: Wow!!

Hi Stephen,

Just letting you know ISA and SIPP at new highs...so far your healthy call has been spot-on!.... one of the funds I chose is up 8.5% (JUPITER UNIT TRUST MANAGERS EMERGING EUROPEAN OPPORTUNITIES FUND).

Kind regards,

Glenn

In case you are wondering, the 8.5% tax-free gain Glenn made was over a 3 week period.

On our website (www.ISACO.co.uk), we have over 100 of our premium clients commenting on our system. If you like, go and take a look.

But how can you personally benefit from this opportunity?

Here's how.

First of all, see if you like the book. If you don't like it you simply do nothing. But let's say that the information you learn really excites you. If it does, Stephen will show you how to take either a "Do It Yourself" or a "Get Help" approach. That's right, you are in complete control. You can either ignore the information (if it does not appeal), run with it on your own (if you like it) or as a final alternative, if you like it and want to make it easier and more time friendly, Stephen will show you how you can personally shadow invest what he is doing with his tax-free money–and it will take you less than 3 minutes per day. This means if he gets a 23% tax-free annual return, so do you.

It really is an amazing opportunity to follow in the footsteps of a high profile investor. And with Stephen being so dedicated and extremely talented at what he does, it is an opportunity that could make you a substantial amount of wealth, and with very little effort on your part.

My suggestion is to read *Liquid Millionaire* as soon as possible–just so that you can rule yourself in or out. If you leave it too late, you might miss out on a possible up and coming stock market boom. I sincerely hope you enjoy this book. I have a feeling it might be the final combination in the lock that you've been looking for.

Who knows, it may even change your life.

Good luck with your investing.

Your friend,

Paul Sutherland.

Managing Director of ISACO.

About the Author

Stephen Sutherland; the UK's Leading Authority in ISA Trend Investing

By combining his expertise in how the stock market works with ISAs, Stephen Sutherland became the creator and pioneer of a brand new way to invest; ISA Trend Investing.

With ISA Trend Investing you trade investment funds (not stocks) using an ISA, a SIPP or both, to achieve tax-free, index beating returns.

You simply profit in up markets and protect in down markets.

Predicted the Start and End of the 2003-2007 Bull Market

Understanding market direction (the trend) helped Stephen correctly predict the start *and* end of the 2003-2007 bull market.

Correctly predicting the start of that 5 year bull market quickly helped him become a "liquid" millionaire.

£19,000 to £783,000 in Just over 3 Years

From May 2000 to July 2003, Stephen's trading account jumped from $31,409 to $1.28 million.

Also, close to the beginning of the new bull market, over a 7 month period he made a £464,634 gain and in just one day, he made a tidy £107,543.

£107,543 "One Day" Scoop Helps
to Buy Dad a Bentley

With this one day gain, he and his brother Paul decided to buy their dad his dream car; a Bentley Continental.

Another big one day win came in on the 13th of October 2008.

That was when Stephen's joint trading account surged 39.3%.

Yes, he scored close to a 40% gain—on his full trading account—in a single day.

How did he do that?

Believe it or not, it happened in a period when most investors were panicking and selling.

Because Stephen saw a huge opportunity, he boldly bet on the market rising and aggressively bought a large number of QQQQ call options; the tracking stock of the Nasdaq 100.

This bold move helped his account post a gain for the month, beating the market by 20.6%.

This was the same month that US stocks suffered their worst monthly losses in 21 years.

BROTHERS WHO MADE STOCK MARKET FORTUNE TREAT FATHER

LUXURY: Paul and Stephen Sutherland with proud parents Brian and Marie and the Bentley Continental

Thanks Dad - and here's your Bentley

TWO Mossley men who made £107,543 in a day on the stock market decided to make their fathers dream come true.

Paul Sutherland 31, and his business partner brother Stephen 34, made the astounding amount trading in stocks and shares - and as their father Brian had always dreamed of owning a Bentley they bought one for him.

Stephen said: "He is the greatest dad you could wish for and because he's helped and supported us all this time. It was our way of showing our appreciation."

As a gift they bought him a Bentley Continental two door coupe. Brian and his wife Marie live at Daisy Nook, Ashton.

The brothers, who left St. Damien's School, Ashton with few qualifications went on to work for the family cleaning and maintenance business, earning only £47 in their first week's wage. However they have been living a success story for several years.

Since 2001 they have been steadily building up their business which has two functions.

Stephen is the stock market wizard who makes profits from investing activities and Paul looks after Fast-Track Education Ltd, teaching people the secrets of how to gain financial independence.

The company operates from their purpose built £300,000 luxury home in Chellow Court, Mossley.

The brothers have also written a book about the fast track to financial independence in which they share ingredients to money making.

Proud parents (Far left) with Stephen (Left) and Paul Sutherland (Right).
Editorial Courtesy of Tameside Advertiser

As well as correctly predicting the start of the powerful five year bull market that began March 2003, he also correctly called the bear market, quickly moving into a cash based fund many months before the 24.7% market falls from Oct 07 to March 2008. That skilful decision helped his clients to preserve and protect their capital in a very challenging period.

When Everybody Was Bullish on China, Stephen Was Bearish

Stephen also predicted the end of the Chinese bull market that violently ended in October 2007 and which so far has corrected a nasty 72.8%.

HIRE CAR™; the Key to Finding the Best of the Best Investment Funds

Stephen also created a unique investment fund screening tool and named it HIRE CAR™. Many of Stephen's clients say HIRE CAR™ is perhaps the most effective investment fund screening tool ever developed.

It is a simple seven step process for finding the best of the best investment funds. HIRE CAR™ found the Number 1 performing fund in 2003 which made a gain of 91.05%.

Champion Funds HIRE CAR™ Uncovered after 2003

HIRE CAR™ went on to help Stephen and his clients find and invest in the Number 1 and the Number 3 top performing funds over the 2003-2007 bull market.

The Number 1 performing fund of the 03-07 bull market is called the Invesco Perpetual Latin America Fund. It gained 587.8%, beating the Nasdaq by almost six times and averaging 47% per year over that 5 year period.

The Number 3 performing fund of the 03-07 bull market is called the Scottish Widows Latin America Fund. This one gained 492.3%, beating the Nasdaq by almost five times and averaging 42.7% per year over that 5 year period.

Through using this unique system of investing, Stephen has personally made a tax-free gain of 1088% over an 11 year period.[16]

Network with Pioneers, Authorities, Sports Stars and Serial Property Investors

Many of Stephen's clients who started with nothing now have six and seven figure accounts. His client list includes aspiring millionaires and multi-millionaires.

His clients come from varied backgrounds and include executives, CEO's, managing directors, business owners, entrepreneurs, pioneers of industries, property investors, sports celebrities and professionals such as doctors, dentists and lawyers.

One of Stephen's clients is the Chair of Trustees who manages a £550 million pound pension fund.

Also on his books are the Chief Information Officer of a FTSE 250 financial company, the original pioneer of health clubs in the UK, a dentist who is a leading authority in cosmetic, implant and restorative dentistry, a professional rugby player, a hedge fund manager and two serial property investors who at the last count owned 150 properties between them.

Stephen is also the co-author of *The FAST TRACK to Financial Independence* which was written in 2001 with his brother Paul. Paul is the Managing Director of ISACO, a company that helps its clients retire rich in just 3 minutes per day.

Living the Dream

In 2007, Stephen and his brother Paul officially became "financially free" (living dream lifestyles). Both Stephen and his brother are still in their thirties.[17]

People who have known Stephen a long time say that although he can be very direct, he is extremely likeable, a real expert in his field and a man of total integrity. Stephen's personal philosophy on "how to live a good life" is based on four key elements; to learn, to serve, to love and to experience.

INTRODUCTION

Wallace D. Wattles, author of the classic *The Science of Getting Rich* once wrote, *"To become really rich is the noblest aim you can have in life, for it includes everything else."*

If your aim is to become *really* rich, you might like what I am about to say.

In this book, you will learn how to make millions in tax-free cash.

But before we go into how it's possible to do that, let me explain who *Liquid Millionaire* is ideally aimed at.

Here is the short and fast answer:

Hungry, ambitious individuals who want to retire rich and have one or more of the following motivations:-

- Financial Security in Retirement.

- A Better Personal Lifestyle.

- Desire to Enjoy the Finer Things in Life.

- Being Able to Travel Extensively.

- Financial Security for the Children.

- Early Retirement.

- Being Able to Afford a Large Property in an Affluent Area.

- Private Education for the Children.

+ The Enjoyment of Making Money.

+ Being Able to Help Others.

+ Status.

+ Owning More Than One Property.

Let me ask you a question.

Did you know that right now, the stock market could be presenting you with a golden opportunity?

It is an opportunity which, if you take full advantage of it, will probably end up making you millions in tax-free cash. The last time you were presented with such a massive opportunity to profit was back in 1980. That was just after the stock market had hardly moved in price for the previous ten year period—and then it took off, advancing 3470% over the next 20 years.[18]

Did you know that if, during the last 10 years, the market had continued in its long-term trend of 18.3%, by the end of 2007, it would have been trading at 8433 instead of 2652?[19]

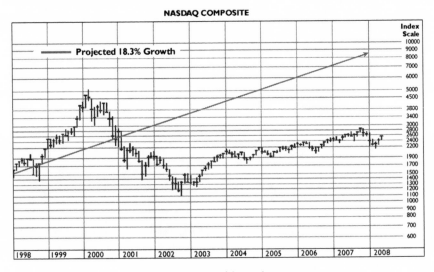

Data Supplied by Yahoo.

Yes, it's true and the investment opportunity you have in front of you is almost identical to the opportunity that the property market was presenting investors back in 1994.[20]

Let me explain. From 1995 to 2006, house prices increased by an incredible 215%.[21] You do not need me to tell you that anybody in the know will have made a killing. You see, property investors in the know were very aware that from 1984 to 1994, property prices moved sideways. These smart investors knew that to purchase property at 1984's prices was a golden investment opportunity.

They knew that over the long-term, property prices ALWAYS go up and because house prices had made no price progress over that decade, it meant that the market was *probably* due a move.

Imagine if you could jump into a time machine, go back to 1994 and make a killing on the property market.

Would that opportunity excite you?

If it would, you might like this. It is a fact that the stock market, just like the property market, is in a long-term uptrend. Take a look at this chart if you do not believe me.

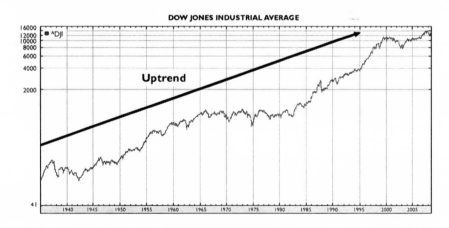

Data Supplied by Yahoo.

But why is it that the stock market keeps moving into new high ground?

In our first book, *The FAST TRACK to Financial Independence*, my brother Paul and I said:

"The reason the stock market keeps going higher is that our world is continually getting better and better. It is a fiercely competitive world that we live in and new exciting and dynamic products and services are being created and developed all the time.

This will always continue to happen and people will continually need to buy products and services just to survive. For example, we will always need food, drink, clothing and shelter.

People will continue to buy from established companies products and services as well as purchasing products and services from new and dynamic companies. Companies will make profits on the goods and services they sell. Investors will always want to buy shares in well-established, deemed safer, companies. Other investors will want to invest their money in new hot growth companies. Stocks prices will continually rise.

The strongest, most innovative companies will survive. The dinosaurs that don't move with the times will die. New companies will replace them. Competition is becoming stronger in each industry every single year.

So let me repeat this key point. The stock market will always continue to rise higher and higher. It will have brief periods when it will correct but it will never stop going higher and higher."

So now you know that just like property prices always eventually go higher, so does the stock market. From time to time, stock and property markets can get ahead of themselves. And when they do, they need to rest and recover whilst they get their breath back before eventually moving higher. This is normal and natural and simply the way markets work.

Here is another fact you might like. The stock market has hardly budged in price over the last decade. In fact, its annual compounded rate of return has been a measly 2.2%.[22] And when you compare the Nasdaq's weak and feeble 2.2% annual growth to its long-term growth rate of 18.3%, you can clearly see that over the last 10 years, it has been seriously under-performing its longer term trend. You will see evidence to prove this point later in the book.

And just like property prices, the stock market can't keep going sideways forever. That means at some point in time, it will have to catch up with its long-term trend.

What does all this mean?

It means, because very little price progress has been made over the last ten years, we could be sitting on the top of a volcano that is ready to erupt.

Will it erupt?

Yes.

When will it erupt?

Possibly very soon, in fact it may have already started. Now that is something to get excited about, especially if you know how you can personally profit from this insight.

This book is about to give you the information on how to capitalise big time. And that knowledge could be the way to help you make a tax-free fortune. Yes, I did say "tax-free," and the amount you could accumulate over the next ten years, depending on where you are starting from, could be in the tens of millions.

Would learning how to make millions in tax-free cash over the next five to ten years interest you?

Would discovering a way to retire with enough money to fund your dream lifestyle appeal?

Are you curious to find out more?

Have you started to get excited?

To say that this investment opportunity is exciting would be the understatement of the century.

But could a person—with no prior knowledge of the stock market—make millions of pounds over the next 5-10 years?

Yes, absolutely.

Are we talking guaranteed?

No; if you are looking for a guarantee then this is not the book for you. But if you are looking for an investment opportunity—and you are the sort of person who likes the concept of *probability*, this book may be for you. And of course, it all depends on where you are starting from.

First of all I need to ask you this question:

Are you a get-rich-quicker looking for a "sure thing?"

If you are, I am sorry but I can not help you.

But what I can help you to do is generate enough liquid capital in your lifetime so that you can retire rich and live a truly amazing, dream lifestyle. My friend, you are about to learn a breakthrough, easy to understand, method of investing using the UK's best-kept secret, the beloved ISA.

Its name is "ISA *TREND* INVESTING."

Now I am sure you have heard of ISA Investing before.

What about trend investing—have you heard of that before?

Hmmm…maybe? But have you heard of ISA Trend Investing?

At this stage, it does not matter if you answered yes or no. But what I can assure you is that this way of using ISAs—to become tax-free wealthy—is a totally new concept. When people ask me to summarise what ISA Trend Investing is, this is what I say:

"With ISA Trend Investing you trade investment funds (not stocks) using an ISA, a SIPP or both, to achieve tax-free, index beating returns. You simply profit in up markets and protect in down markets."

Now before we take a look at the 7 elements that make this way of investing in ISAs different, I want to give you a taster of what trend investing is and we can start this by clarifying what the term trend actually means when it is related to investing.

Answers.com in their Investment Dictionary section had this to say:[23]

"If you can identify a trend, it can be highly profitable, because you will be able to trade with the trend."

And InvestorDictionary.com had this to say about trend investing:[24]

"…success depends on identifying the trend with confidence and catching the trend after it has started. Success includes getting out of the trend as soon as possible after the uptrend turns into a downtrend."

Unfortunately financial advisers, stock brokers and banks do not help individuals to invest in ISAs in this way. They do not inform you of trend changes.

Did you know that the market is officially "healthy" when it's in an uptrend? Yes, it's true, and later on in this book you are going to be finding out why uptrends are ALWAYS the best and safest time to invest.

When the market is officially in an uptrend (bull market), advisers, brokers and banks *should* be informing their clients to invest. On the other hand, when the market is in a downtrend (bear market), advisers *should* be informing their clients not to invest.[25]

To clarify, I am not saying this is easy to do. All I am saying is that it's possible—if you know what you are doing. The reason advisers, stock brokers and banks do not give their clients this information is because they simply do not know how. To put it another way, they are unable to accurately read the direction or trend of the market.

You see, reading future market direction is a skill that has to be developed over time. Advisers, brokers and banks simply never receive the correct training to acquire this key skill. And most never will. That is the reason why, when they put you in an investment, you do not hear from them again for a long time. Of course, they keep taking their commissions, but you still never seem to hear from them again.

Have you noticed that they never inform you of important trend changes in the market?

It's true isn't it?

And because of this, many private individuals end up losing a lot of money—losses that could have easily been avoided. Financial advisers, stock brokers and banks are therefore only trained in how to sell products and how financial products work.

The people who truly understand the market and which way the market is heading (trend) are <u>successful stock market professionals</u>. Stock market professionals are people who invest in the market for a living. This means they are doing it all the time. They watch the market every day. They do not sell stocks, investment funds or other financial products to clients. Instead, they invest in the market; period.

And the successful ones, the top ten percent, are the ones who not only make 80% of all the money, but also the ones that *you* want to be following. These people are the ones who can help you to invest with the trend....and win.

And keeping with this theme of trend investing, professional investor and author Mark Shipman in his excellent book; *The Next Big Investment Boom* had this to say:

"It is no coincidence that the hedge funds and other alternative investment companies that employ trend following strategies are responsible for some of the most spectacular performance returns."

In other words, you can make some serious money if you know how to invest with the trend.

Before we move on, let me just clear something up. The comments I made earlier with regard to what advisers, brokers and banks *should* be doing, is of course a personal opinion of mine. And I may have it all wrong. But it was interesting to see that in the wealth section of the June 21st/June 22nd 2008 edition of the *Financial Times*, there was an article that helped to confirm my thoughts and beliefs. The headline read, *"Wealthy want more bank for their buck"* with the sub-headline *"Large numbers of well-off investors are unhappy with their managers and advisers."*

The article, written by Matthew Vincent, mentioned that more than a third of wealthy investors are considering changing their private bank to get a better service, and half are thinking of changing their investment managers.

I don't think I need to go into the article in great detail for you to get the idea. This is just another example highlighting the fact that many high net worth investors are not happy about the levels of service they receive from their advisers.

However, at the end of the day, we have to remember that it's all about *results*. You want to be teamed up with a person who can deliver the goods year in, year out. In other words, if your financial adviser, broker or bank's advice has helped you to *beat* the market over the long-term, you've found yourself an outstanding contact. But if he or she has not helped you to beat the market over the long-term, it may be time to look for an alternative.

And the good news is that by the end of this book, you will understand exactly how to read the trend of the market—and why it is so vital to your success—to know the trend or direction that the market is heading in. In other words, when you have finished reading *Liquid Millionaire*, you will understand when to get into the market and when to get out. And because advisers, brokers and banks do not tell you this absolutely essential information, if you follow their advice, you might end up seriously underperforming the market and in a worse case scenario, failing to hit the financial retirement goals you've set for yourself.

Okay, its time to get really clear on this brand new way of ISA Investing.

When compared to normal ISA Investing, the 7 key differences are:

1. Instead of simply buying and holding, you are *active*. By understanding the overall trend or direction of the market, you invest into the market when the confirmation of the trend is up, and switch out of the market when the confirmation of the trend is down. This is the most important element in ISA Trend Investing.

This first difference is the one that will lead you to success if you get it right or failure if you get it wrong. Even if you find the best investment fund on the planet, if your trend reading is wrong, meaning your timing is wrong, you will fail.

2. You use a Stocks and Shares ISA instead of a Cash ISA.

3. When the trend is confirmed up, you look to buy the highest quality *Investment Funds*. You search for funds that can be purchased within a Stocks and Shares ISA. You do not buy individual stocks as they carry too much risk. You do not buy index tracker funds because it is possible to "beat" the indexes if you know what you are doing. You buy your fund

or funds only when the market is healthy (uptrend). When the market is unhealthy (downtrend), you remain in a cash based fund.

4. When the market is healthy you time your buying of the fund or funds that you have selected. You only buy your fund or funds at the time where there is the maximum probability of success. To do this, you use technical analysis or charts.

5. You time your exits. When the market's trend is in a confirmed downtrend, **instead of selling and cashing in your ISA, you <u>switch</u>.** This helps you to move out of the downtrend so that you are completely out of the market. This means your cash is now placed or "parked" in a Stocks and Shares cash based fund. You do this as soon as the market confirms its downtrend meaning the market is now unhealthy and unsafe to invest. This helps you to bank profits and *protect* and *preserve* your capital whilst the market is falling.

6. Because you can read the trend of the market, *and* pick the highest quality investment funds, it allows you to set yourself aggressive performance targets. You aim to beat the powerful US Nasdaq Composite. (The Nasdaq is capable of 24.5% annual returns over the long-term.)[26]

7. You do not use an adviser. You become your own adviser and make your trades on a "smart" investing platform with virtually zero costs. By being your own adviser, you save on charges, commissions and initial set up fees. This seriously helps boost your overall compounded returns. And if you know what you are doing, you get much better results than you would if you were with an adviser.

With this method of investing in ISAs you also have the option of:

1) "Shadow" Investing successful ISA Trend Investors.[27] This allows you to get exactly the same returns as they are getting and in a time friendly way.

2) SIPP Trend Investing. A SIPP (Self Invested Personal Pension) can be run parallel with your ISA Trend Investing. Whichever investment fund you buy with your ISA, you buy the same fund

with your SIPP. That means if you get a 20% annual return on your ISA, you get a 20% annual return on your SIPP.

Would you like to know what others have to say about trend investing?

Good.

Let's start with Dan Denning, author of *The Bull Hunter*. Dan said, *"The sun never really goes down on investors who look for good value and invest along with powerful trends."*

High profile commodities trader Ed Seykota was quoted as saying, *"All profitable systems trade trends."*

Finally, multi-billion dollar trend following investment manager John W. Henry said, *"Perhaps the investment philosophy that makes the most sense, if you study the implications carefully, is trend following."*

Now it is time to talk ISAs.

ISAs are incredible.

But the majority of people living in the UK simply do not know how powerful ISAs are. It simply isn't common knowledge.

Were you aware that ISAs can help you accumulate a multi-million pound, tax-free portfolio?

Yes, it's true, but the thing is, to win with ISAs you need to know how to create much better returns than you can get on the high street from banks and building societies. To put it another way, you need to stay away from Cash ISAs and instead use Stocks and Shares ISAs to build your tax-free fortune.

As bestselling author Robert Allen once stated, *"How many millionaires do you know who have become wealthy by investing in savings accounts? I rest my case."*

But here is a quick word of warning. Even though ISA Trend Investing is a great way to help you reach financial security, you should not view ISA Trend Investing as the ultimate panacea. This type of investing should supplement other strategies to build your wealth. It is very risky to rely on just one way to secure your future.

ISA Trend Investing should therefore be viewed as just *one* of the essential parts of your overall wealth building strategy. You will learn more about what the other parts are in Chapter 9 when you discover "The Ultimate Wealth Building Model."

Because of the huge tax-free advantages that come with ISA Investing, the first £7,200 (£14,400 in total if you have a partner) that you are planning to invest should ALWAYS go into your ISA account. Any money that you have over and above that amount can be wisely invested into other assets.

When reading this book, feel free to drink deeply from whichever chapter takes your fancy. If you want to quickly make a decision about whether this book is ideally suited to you, I suggest reading Chapters 4 and 5. But please be aware that skimming over these two fact-filled chapters is not the best of ideas. You see, it's vital you really digest the information if your goal is to make good financial decisions going forward.

If you really want to get the best from this book, my recommendation would be to read it in the order it's written. But to make this even easier for you, a summary of each chapter is provided right here in the introduction. This book has been written in a way that helps to build up your knowledge of "How to Retire Rich" one step at a time and it has been created with two things in mind; to be easy to read and thoroughly enjoyable.

The full book can be read from cover to cover over a weekend—or a week at the most. I thoroughly recommend you allocate some quiet time to read it—after all, what you learn could lead to a life of Financial Freedom.

So let's talk about each chapter to see if it's going to be worth your while reading it. Let's start with a question in relation to Chapter 1.

Would you like to know how you could turn $31,409 into $1.28 million in just over 3 years?

If you would, you'll be happy to know that in this juicy chapter, you get a complete timeline of exactly how I did it. And if stock trading appeals to you, the information you will gather from this chapter will show you how to fast track towards liquid riches.

Would you like to learn a foolproof way to create your dream lifestyle?

And faster than you could ever imagine?

If you answered yes, Chapter 2 will get you sitting up in your chair.

Would discovering a sure-fire way to know how much money you are likely to make in <u>any</u> given period of time interest you?

If it would, then Chapter 3 might very well be what you've been searching for.

Does learning how it is possible to make up to 30% returns over the next 10 years get your heart racing?

If you said yes, you will like Chapter 4.

Would knowing how it's possible to make millions from a potential up and coming stock market boom give you a feeling of exhilaration?

Then Chapter 5 is going to get your heart pumping.

Is time a big factor in your life? Is your goal to retire rich by putting in the least amount of effort?

If it is, then you and I are very much alike. And you are probably a big believer in making things easier for yourself.

So am I.

And that tells me you will probably get a serious buzz from Chapter 6.

Did you know there is one skill that if mastered, will open the vault to unlimited riches?

Yes, it's true, and that valuable skill is fully disclosed in Chapter 7. This is the chapter where you learn how to read the market like a pro. And once you can analyse and interpret which way the stock market is heading, it's like receiving a licence to print money. Miss this one at your peril.

Do you have a goal to make more than a million? Would you like to know how you can be remembered as a hero?

If yes, Chapter 8 will be just your bag. In this thrilling chapter, you will learn how your first million could end up ballooning into a mouth-watering £75 million. And you will also discover things that could seriously extend your life expectancy, helping to give you much more time to really enjoy your riches.

Have you ever heard the term *Life Extension?*

Do you want to know what technology has in store for us all in the future?

I can assure you that the future looks warm, kind and glowing with goodness—and you learn all about it in this electrifying chapter.

And what do I have in store for the finale?

Drum roll please.

In Chapter 9, you are introduced to something very special. I call it "The Ultimate Wealth Building Model." If you want to turbo-boost your plan for achieving your financial goals, this chapter will be a real treat. If this chapter doesn't get you fired up, then you may be ready for the oblong box with lily in hand. It's absolutely oozing with goodies and it really helps to bring everything you have learned together in a gripping completion to the book.

Oh, and if you are a person who likes to get valuable things for free, don't forget to take a look at page xxv. That's the BONUS section which tells you how you can quickly get your hands on 3 FREE Special Wealth Building Reports with a recommended retail price of £497.

But why give close to £500 worth of product away for free? What is the catch?

There is no catch. The reason I decided to do this is because if you like the information found in the special reports, you may end up one day becoming a client. Of course, the information is not going to appeal to everybody but you just might be one of those people who love it. And if you came on board, and joined our club, that would be a win for both you and me.

Just so that you are aware, you are going to hear many things repeated in this book. If something is mentioned on more than one occasion, there is a very good reason behind it. For example, there are certain principles about how the market works that are absolutely critical for you to understand. By me repeating them again and again and again, it will help them sink deep into your subconscious.

When these concepts burrow deep, your overall understanding of how the system works will grow. Your confidence will start to spiral upwards which in turn will help create the two key beliefs of "I *can* do this" and "I *will* one day be Financially Free."

This in turn will maximize your probability of retiring rich.

And there is just one more thing. As Paul mentioned before, at the end of this book you will have a choice of three routes to take.

The first route is that you don't like what is presented to you. In which case we take things no further, part company and wish each other well.

The second route, if you like what you learn, will be to take what I call a "DIY" or "Do It Yourself" approach. You might finish the book and be thinking something along the lines of … *"I really like this and can see the opportunity but I have decided that I will not need your help because I reckon I would be able to do this myself"* … and off you go on your merry way. If you do that, it's fine by me and I am glad to have helped you start on your journey.

However, the third and final route is to invest in expert help. I call this the "Get Help" approach. This is when you not only like the concept and the investment opportunity presented—but you also love the way you can shadow invest what I am doing with my money and get the same returns as me.

By simply plugging into my knowledge of how the stock market works, you increase the probability of retiring rich and in just 3 minutes per day.

But I have to warn you…this third route is not for everybody and I will be explaining who it is ideally suited for later in the book.

And I promise that I'll make it very clear why our shadow investing system takes just 3 minutes per day. For example, you'll learn that the information you receive daily, allowing you to shadow invest me, takes less than 3 minutes to read. This means when I get a 23% tax-free return, so do you—and in an extremely time friendly way.

But why is it that some people want to shadow invest me?

It might be because of my past performance.

One of my claims to fame, so to speak, is that I turned $31,409 into $1.28 million in 38 months.[28]

Would you like to know how I did it?

Good, because now is the time for sharing with you…

CHAPTER 1

How I Turned $31,409 into $1.28 Million in 38 Months

"If you want to master the art of wealth building—so you can become financially independent and create wealth automatically whenever and wherever you want to—you need to learn wealth building the way any master learns his art: by repeating, as closely as possible, the actions of successful wealth builders."
– Michael Masterson

The reason I decided to share how I turned $31,409 into $1.28 million over a 38 month period is two fold. The first reason is because people are naturally curious and simply want to know exactly how I did it. The second reason is to introduce you to <u>the timing system</u> that my clients and I use to trend invest. Trend investing helps you to move into and out of the market at the right time.

Get in on Strength and Out on Weakness

This timing system, that allows you to get in on strength and out on weakness, is not flawless—but as you are about to discover, **it has managed to catch the start of every single bull (up) market in the last 50 years.**[29] Amongst its many other triumphs, it also helped my clients to *protect* and *preserve* their profits in the bear market that started in the last quarter of 2007.

Let's start the story with some brief background information.

An "F" in Maths

I was born in 1968. During my school years, I did poorly, leaving at age sixteen with just one CSE grade one qualification. In Maths I remember getting an "F."

Subsequently I said no to college and university and instead went to work for my Dad as an apprentice painter and decorator. My weekly wage was less than £50. Dad is a self-made man who started and built a successful cleaning and maintenance business. In 1987, when I was 19, Dad started to teach me how a business worked. This was all part of his grand plan of passing on the business to me. Over the next 10 years, I dug in and learned all I could about how to manage a successful business.

In 1998, I was primed and ready to take the reigns. And I knew that if I wanted to take the family business to the next level, I was going to need some expert help.

The Telephone Call That Changed the Whole Direction of My Life

I remember receiving a telephone call from a marketing company called Results Corporation. The chap who called me said his company had a proven way to grow small businesses. I remember being totally enthused by their ideas and I loved their overall philosophy.

Their philosophy was simply this: *Learn from the experts.*

Shortly after teaming up with Results, we started receiving monthly newsletters and in those newsletters were book recommendations.

I have to be honest, I had not read a book since school, but these book recommendations had really juicy titles. I just had to take a look at them to find out what they were all about. One of the books they recommended was a personal development book written by success guru Tony Robbins. It was called *Awaken the Giant Within*. I loved it so much that I immediately bought my brother Paul a copy. He also read it cover to cover—and loved it just as much as I did. That was where our new journey began.

Success Leaves a Trail

It was around this point we both discovered that to achieve any goal, you simply had to model the experts.

As Anthony Robbins once said, *"If you want to be successful, find someone who has achieved the results you want and copy what they do and you'll achieve the same results."*

And as Canadian psychologist and author Albert Bandura wrote, *"The most effective way of transmitting information about a skill is through proficient modelling."*

To put it another way, if you want to be a big success in cookery, simply study the best chefs in the world and emulate their techniques. It was also around this time that I awoke to the realisation that in life, there are no action replays. I remember starting to think more clearly about what I wanted from my life. And soon I realised that Dad's cleaning and maintenance business was not what I wanted.

I discovered that my true vocation was somehow connected to the stock market. I had been listening to a lot of personal development authors talking on the subject of getting on purpose. Robert Allen's wise words, *"Pursuing your passion is fulfilling and leads to Financial Freedom,"* really made an impact on how I was thinking about my future.

And so I started to ask myself questions such as:

What would be your dream job?

What work would you love to do even if you weren't paid?

What job would give you your greatest feeling of importance?

The answers to these questions all seemed to centre on becoming a full-time stock market professional because I had always had a keen interest in the stock market right from an early age.

A Serious Passion for the Stock Market

I had two goals. The first was to become an outstanding professional stock market investor. The second was to help others achieve their financial goals by sharing with them the secrets of my success. The thrill of becoming a full-time stock market professional was immensely compelling but I knew that I would have to prove to myself and others that I was excellent at what I was doing if I was going to achieve both of my objectives. To do this, I knew I would have to produce truly outstanding results. I considered this Stage One in my long-term plan.

Once I had proved to myself and others that I was a leading authority on the stock market, I could then move on to Stage Two of my plan; to help others learn the skills I had mastered. I knew that if I could create outstanding results, people would take me seriously and seek my help and advice. I knew in advance that this would be incredibly rewarding.

My plan to achieve the two goals was simple; Learn from the best.

Mr William O'Neil; a Leading Stock Market Authority with 50 years Experience

You could say that my objective of becoming a stock market professional began in 1999. After attending a four day wealth building seminar in Oct 1999,[30] one of the speakers,[31] a professional investor, kept referring to Bill O'Neil.

I had never heard of Bill O'Neil at the time, but because of the numerous references to him, I knew I would have to check him out after the seminar was over.

I found to my delight that Bill O'Neil was a leading authority on the stock market with over 50 years experience.[32] In fact, Bill's past results meant that he would be an absolutely perfect person to model to help me achieve my goals.

Not Missed the Start of __EVERY__ Bull Market in the Last 50 Years

I soon discovered that O'Neil was a living stock market legend who had a proven 50 year system of investing that worked in good times and bad.

Of course, I was a little sceptical at first, but when I delved deeper and learned that with his system, he had not missed the start of every single bull (up trending) market in the last 50 years,[33] I was sold.

What added to my belief were his trading results. I discovered he made a 2000% plus gain on his portfolio in just 26 months.[34] I thought, wow, this guy must really know what he is doing.

Total Immersion Was the Key

Albert Einstein once said, *"Only one who devotes himself to a cause with his whole strength and soul can be a true master. For this reason mastery demands all of a person."*

I decided to totally immerse myself in O'Neil's philosophy on investing. I aggressively read all of O'Neil's books, all the books O'Neil had read, listened intently to all of his audio programmes and eventually I started to subscribe to O'Neil's premium equity research package.[35] I also flew across the Atlantic twice to see Bill in person as part of my learning programme. I first saw him speak in 2001 in South Beach, Miami. The second time I saw him was in New York in 2002.[36]

But what exactly happened?

How did I turn $31,409 into $1.28 million?

The best way to explain what happened is to use a time line:

- After reading O'Neil's book *How to Make Money in Stocks* (about three or four times), I started to paper trade the market. In case you have not heard of the term before, paper trading is simulated trading that investors use to practice mimicking trades (buys and sells) without actually entering into any monetary transactions. Paper trading is a good way to learn the ropes without risking any money. You can do it simply by pretending to buy and sell stock and keep notes of paper profits or losses.

- As soon as I gained confidence, I set up a trading account with a brokerage company called Ameritrade–with a starting amount of $31,409. This was in May 2000.

- Little did I know that I had just started my stock investing apprenticeship at a time when the market had just begun what was going to be known as one of the worst bear (down) markets in the stock market's entire history.

- Every time I got a confirmation that the trend was up, I started to trade using O'Neil's CAN SLIM™ formula as my guide. The key was to use really small amounts and always keep tight 7% stop losses on each and every trade. A stop loss is simply a point below your buy price that you've decided to sell. This meant that if a stock I owned dropped 7% below my buy price, I would sell it immediately. By doing this, I knew that I would have to make literally hundreds of bad trades to lose all my starting capital. That gave me confidence to take my time and create good investment habits.

- The rallies that I was trading turned out to be *bear market rallies* which meant that after a period of between a few weeks and several months, the rally became a downtrend. In case you are not familiar with the term rally, it is simply a rise in the price of an individual security or in the market as a whole.

- As these rallies turned into downtrends, I was forced out onto the sidelines into the safety of cash. This meant I sold all the stocks I owned which in turn helped me to raise capital. I did this until all my money in my portfolio was in cash. This meant I was officially out of the market.

- Whilst waiting on the sidelines in cash, I had to patiently sit tight for another confirmation of a rally. A valid confirmation came from various indicators such as how the main indexes were acting and how leading stocks were behaving. By the way, you will learn more about how to confirm if a market is deemed safe to invest in Chapter 7.

- The study and countless hours slowly started to pay off. Unbelievably, that first year (2000), my account actually saw a gain. Even though I made very little money, I somehow managed to beat the market by 40.6%.[37]

- This first year's result fuelled me to get even more aggressive with my personal development–plus I increased the amount of hours that I was devoting to the market.

- In January 2001, I went to see my mentor and hero Bill O'Neil. Bill was speaking in Miami and what I learned from him seriously increased my overall knowledge and understanding of how the market really works.

- At this seminar, I remember my beliefs about what was possible getting smashed. For example, O'Neil explained that some of his money managers were making between 100% and 600% gains in a single year.

- In 2001, the second year of what is now known as probably the worst bear market in history, I managed to return 31.74% beating the Nasdaq index by 52.79%.[38]

- I was shocked but also delighted to learn that my 2001 return beat the Number 1 UK fund manager Ashley Willing who was managing a fund called Gartmore UK Focus which incidentally was an investment fund that returned 13.72% for the year.[39] This success of mine spurred me on even further and helped give my confidence as an investor a serious boost.

- In January 2002, I flew over to New York to see O'Neil again. My knowledge deepened.

- In October the same year I recognised that the market had found a bottom, but I did not jump in until I was absolutely certain that the great bear market was over.

- Because I had learned that the big money was always made in the first two years of a new bull market,[40] I decided to contact my bank manager to ask if the bank would consider lending me £1 million pounds. Seriously, I asked if I could borrow £1 million pounds.

- My bank manager thought I had lost the plot. He said, "Do you know that the US and Iraq are in conflict and a war could soon erupt? What if Saddam Hussein uses chemical and biological warfare?"

9

- Undeterred due to my conviction that something big was about to happen, I moved to Plan B which was to raise cash by equity releasing money from our home.

- Because of my absolute certainty and belief in my abilities, I decided to bet the ranch. This was also based on my concrete belief that we had just entered a brand new bull market. After all, highly successful stock investor and philanthropist George Soros did once say: *"If your investment is going well, follow your instincts and go with all you've got."*

- The money I was using to trade with belonged to a joint account. And so I had to convince my brother Paul that it would be a sound idea to release close to quarter of a million pounds from our home. Paul backed me all the way.

- In May 2003, I took the money from the equity release and wired it to my trading account. This amounted to $416,472.90.

- I was right about my prediction that a new bull market had begun.[41] My decision to raise the money and get it into the market started to pay off.

- Early on in the bull run, I latched onto three beauties which I later named "The Three Amigos." They were three white hot Chinese internet stocks with stock ticker symbols SINA, NTES and SOHU.

- My formula for picking the best stocks was right on the money. These 3 companies turned out to be probably the 3 biggest winning stocks of the 2003-2007 bull market. SINA made a gain of 4753% in 27 months,[42] SOHU jumped 8246% in 27 months[43] and NTES surged 13746%, again over a 27 month period.[44]

- By investing heavily into these stocks and using leverage from Ameritrade *and* day trading buying power (even more leverage), it helped me to control over $2 million worth of stock.

- I used sound trading rules and a huge amount of leverage, to buy The Three Amigos. I started to buy them when they were in safe price ranges (approximately $15.00).

- I made sure that I bought the Amigos as they broke out of sound constructive bases. In case you are wondering, a base is a term used by investors to refer to a resting period in a stock's chart pattern. This resting period is called consolidation. When a stock consolidates, it typically can be an indicator for future price advances. This price consolidation pattern generally lasts around seven weeks but can last as long as twelve months.

- I bought large amounts of stock from each of the three companies plus I also day traded each of them. Day trading is when you buy and sell a stock on the very same day.

- By July 2003, NTES had jumped to $50.46. SINA had surged to $34.76 and SOHU had bolted to $39.74, helping my portfolio to bank some pretty good gains.

- On the 10th of July, the account was valued at $1,284, 826.94 (approximately £783,000).

- This meant that I had made $761,661 (approximately £464,634), which equated to a 145.6% gain in just 7 months[45] with the biggest one day move coming in on the 10th July 2003. This one day gain gave me a 16.12% rise on my portfolio.

This was the day I made the £107,543 used to buy our Dad his dream car; a Bentley Continental. Not wanting to leave mum out, Paul and I bought her a gold and diamond encrusted necklace. When we told our parents of our plan they were totally caught off guard.

I will never forget the looks on their faces and we all became very emotional. It took some time for what I had achieved to really sink in. To have gone from failing at almost every subject in school to being able to provide my parents with the gifts of their dreams felt incredible.

Of course at this point I was totally sold on the timing system. It had not only caught the beginning of every bull market in the last 50 years, it had also helped my brother Paul and I become officially Financially Independent.[46]

Did I Stop Investing to Build a Business?

You might be interested to know if I stopped investing after I hit the magic million. The answer is no. As you may recall, the second half of my plan was to help as many people as I could to realise their financial dreams—and the best way to do that would be through concentrating on building a business.

Earl Nightingale, pioneer of the personal development industry once said, *"Our rewards will always be in exact proportion to our service."*

So Paul and I decided to put a lot of our wealth back into building a business to be proud of.

But there was no way that I was going to stop trading. So as we built the business, I also continued to invest. In 2004 I made some decent profits on a couple of trades. One was a company called Silicon Image Inc (Ticker symbol - SIMG) where I made a quick profit of 24.5% in just two weeks. I also bought the Internet exchange traded fund (Ticker symbol - HHH) and made 30.5% over a six week period.

2005 was a good year that spawned a few winners. Google Inc (Ticker symbol - GOOG) was bought in 2005 but sold in 2006. I made 129.4% over a thirteen week period with that one.

Marvel the Marvellous

But my biggest winner of 2005 was a company called Marvel Technology Group (Ticker symbol – MRVL) which, like Google, was bought in 2005 but sold in 2006. With Marvel, I made 155.6% in twelve weeks. I called it Marvel the Marvellous.

Akami Technologies (Ticker symbol - AKAM) was another company I purchased in 2005 and sold in 2006. With Akami, I made a profit of 68.3% in eleven weeks.

And the other stocks that I owned, sold and made a profit on in 2005 were KOS Pharmaceuticals Inc (Ticker symbol - KOSP) 97.2% in four weeks, Hovnanian Enterprises (Ticker symbol - HOV) 54.6% in five weeks, Semiconductor ETF (Ticker symbol - SMH) 22.1% in five weeks, Sirius Satellite Radio (Ticker symbol - SIRI) 32.4% in two weeks, Genentech Inc (Ticker symbol - DNA) 18.6% in two weeks and Apple Inc (Ticker symbol - AAPL) 21.8% in one week.

Ice Is Cool

In 2006, I picked three of my biggest winners since I began professional investing. My biggest winner in 2006 was a company called Intercontinental Exchange (Ticker symbol - ICE). In fifteen weeks, I made a cool profit of 268%. Las Vegas Sands Corp (Ticker symbol - LVS) was another big winner for me gaining 96% over a seventeen week period. Baidu.com Inc (Ticker symbol - BIDU) was my other success story that year. Baidu is the Chinese equivalent of Google and I made a profit of 158.6% in seven weeks.

Because of market conditions, I did not trade in 2007 and even though 2008 was nasty, I was fortunate to land a huge 39.3% jump on our portfolio– in just one day (13th October).

What I Have Learned about Building Wealth Quickly

You may be wondering how I made these decent gains over such a short space of time.

The answer is *leverage*.

When asked about leverage, billionaire commodity trader Paul Tudor Jones remarked, *"I have always been a big believer in leverage."* And bestselling author Robert Kiyosaki once stated, *"Leverage is power."*

You see, instead of buying the stock, I bought the option. Options provide leverage and are much more risky than stocks and I suggest should only be used if you have mastered stock picking. You can make big money buying options but you can also lose big money too.

Why I Love the Market

Many people want to know how many hours I have put into learning my craft. Since 1999 my best estimate is over 20,000 hours and of course, this number keeps increasing week on week. The market is a complex puzzle—and I love to try to solve it. What fascinates me about the market is that it is forever showing different sides to its personality. It always keeps you on your toes and is continually teaching you new lessons.

As bestselling author David McCullough once said, *"Real success is finding your lifework in the work that you love."*

And that is what I had done. I had made my lifework work I loved. I remember that in the first three or four years, I was putting in at least 70-100 hours per week on the market, in the form of studying, trading, money management and regular reviews of how I was doing. And there is no way I would have done that unless I really did adore my profession. Now my working week is more like 60-70 hours and my love for the market seems to strengthen each and every day. Even when on holiday, I can't keep my eyes off the market. Some people might say I'm obsessed with it, and maybe they are right.

The Idea of "ISA Trend Investing" Is Conceived

I will never forget the day I excitedly realised how this timing system could be used for ISA Investing. When buying individual stocks, with the timing system, the downside was the fact that when you got out you had tax to pay on your gain.

That hurt your compounded returns. And so when I realised you could do this getting in and getting out without paying tax, I was thrilled.

This is when my idea of Trend Investing using ISAs was born. I realised that by using an ISA you could make gains when the market was in an uptrend and then bank those profits—without paying any tax—when the market trend changed. And that is when it suddenly dawned on me what a huge impact that would have in helping boost your annual compounded returns. To top it all, <u>instead of investing in single stocks, it would work much better if you invested in investment funds</u> which I believe are not as risky as stocks but just as powerful.

So there you have it.

The key for me was to find a proven system (CAN SLIM™), master it, start small and then when the time was right, to bet the ranch and use as much leverage that I could get my hands on. The lesson here is, if you know what you are doing, leverage can make you seriously wealthy.

As Archimedes famously said, "*Give me a lever long enough and a fulcrum on which to place it, and I shall move the world.*"

Now it's time to move on. If you are like my clients, your aim is to generate a certain level of wealth that in turn will help you to live your dream lifestyle.

Is that what you are trying to do?

If so, you might be interested in knowing what kind of lifestyle this book can help you to create. If you would, you are probably going to get pretty excited with the next chapter. Let's go and see...

CHAPTER 2

How This Book Can Help You Create Your Dream Lifestyle

"Man, alone, has the power to transform his thoughts into physical reality; man, alone, can dream and make his dreams come true."
- Napoleon Hill

It is most people's dream to be able to create a life that is ideal or perfect in every way. Having enough money will always play a major role in making your dream a reality. By reading *Liquid Millionaire*, you will learn how to set things up in a way that allows you to withdraw tax-free cash that will in turn pay for your dream lifestyle.

And the good news is that when you follow the 7% withdrawal formula, your lifestyle will get dreamier each and every year and you will also become richer each year too. And as you will find out later, your first liquid million could turn into £75 million–if you know what you are doing.

With a Firm Decision, It Is Going to Happen

When starting off on the journey to retire rich, it all begins with making a *commitment*.

Commitments are powerful. In the *Oxford Dictionary of English*, it says that a commitment is *"a dedication to a cause."* And when you are dedicated to a cause, when the going gets tough, which it will, you stubbornly refuse to throw in the towel.

And it's that very resolute attitude that is needed to ensure you keep on going when life throws at you countless challenges, problems and obstacles. When *committed* to retiring Financially Free, you never give up no matter what. You embrace the challenges, you solve the problems and you go around or over the obstacles. And by making your determined behaviour a deeply ingrained habit, you eventually become unstoppable.

Have you made a commitment that you are going to make it, no matter what happens?

To make a commitment, it has to start with a decision.

Ralph Waldo Emerson once said, *"Once you make a decision, the universe conspires to make it happen."*

And once you have made the all important, never go back decision–that one day you will be Financially Free–your next step is to take complete and utter *responsibility* for making that goal a reality.

When you are responsible, there is no blaming, complaining or finger pointing. You decide that the goal is down to you and you alone. And once you have made the decision that you are responsible, great things will start to happen. Your outlook on life will change dramatically.

You will develop an attitude of, if this is going to happen, it is down to me and me alone.

One of the keys to success that I learned from bestselling author and international speaker Brian Tracy was to simply make good on the decisions and promises we make to ourselves. It sounds simple doesn't it, but when you think about it, it's extremely profound.

And so once that big decision has been made, the next step is to gain absolute *clarity* on what it is that you want and by when. This helps to create *desire* and it is desire that will help to create a tremendous pull towards your intended goal.

When I speak to prospective clients, some of them are not clear about what they want to achieve. Not being clear on your financial goal is like not knowing where your end destination is when looking at a map. And if a person is a little fuzzy on what they want, I help them to gain clarity.

You see, by getting clear on what your dream life will look, sound and feel like when you arrive, it helps to…

1) Create the desire and initial motivation to get started AND to keep going when the going gets tough.

2) Maximize the probability of you eventually arriving at your intended goal.

Why would your probability of success increase just by getting clear on what it is that you want?

In *The New Psycho-Cybernetics*; a classic book that has sold over 30 million copies, the great Maxwell Maltz says that our minds operate like an automatic, goal striving machine.[47]

He calls this goal striving machine your Automatic Success Mechanism (ASM).

Maltz states:

...*"You have an awesomely powerful computer-like success machine at your disposal. Your physical brain and nervous system make up a servo-mechanism that you use and that operates very much like a computer; a mechanical goal seeking device."*[48]

Maltz also said:

"You accelerate personal development and goal achievement by providing your ASM with a clear, precisely detailed, vividly imagined and perfectly communicated "target." As the target gets clearer, the ASM responds by doing its job more efficiently."[49]

A good way to think about this is to imagine the mind being like a self-guided torpedo that, once it knows the coordinates of its target, locks onto it and moves rapidly towards it.

And here is another way to put it. The mind acts like a giant magnet. Whatever you think about, whatever you dwell upon (ie; your ideal vision of the future) is drawn towards you and you towards it. And if you take the necessary action, your thoughts (ie; pictures of your dream lifestyle) end up becoming your physical reality. And so it's important that we try to keep our minds focused on the things we want and off the things we don't want.

Many years ago Earl Nightingale wrote and recorded a message called *The Strangest Secret*–which went on to win a prestigious golden globe award. The strangest secret was, *"You become what you think about most of the time."*

Marcus Aurelius, the great Roman Emperor, said, *"A man's life is what his thoughts make of it."*

And many centuries ago, Buddha stated, *"All that we are is the result of what we have thought."*

Get Crystal Clear on What You Want

You need to get crystal clear on the amount you would need to live for <u>one year</u> of your dream lifestyle. This helps you to calculate the total amount of money you would need to make your ideal lifestyle a reality. This total becomes your Golden Goose. The Golden Eggs that your goose lays is the cash flow that your total sum can pay you each and every year. This is achieved by using a draw down facility that we will talk about later.

Do you know how much cash you would need to enable you to live one year of your ideal or dream lifestyle?

To determine how much money you require, you first of all need to know in detail how your life will look, sound and feel when you have finally attained your goal. You could say that you have to be literally obsessed with attaining your dream lifestyle–because when you want it more than anything, you are much more likely to let nothing get in your way of eventually achieving it.

The more reasons you have, the more desire and the greater the intensity of motivation. And the more you keep stacking the reasons, the greater the power that is created. And once you have momentum, you will literally be like a supercharged freight train thundering down the track with nothing to stop you from attaining your dreams.

So just in case you are unsure, let me help you become clear about how much money you are going to need to live your dream lifestyle. For some people, living a dream lifestyle would require £100,000 per year, but for others this would be too much, and for others not nearly enough.

How much would one year of your dream lifestyle cost you?

I suggest that you fill in the amount below or write it down on a piece of paper.

Your Dream Lifestyle = £_____ per year.

And remember, as Johann Wolfgang von Goethe once said:

"Dream no small dreams for they have no power to move the hearts of men."

Before we move on, now is a good time to explain why committing a goal down on paper is so important in helping you to get what you want. A goal not written down is merely a wish or fantasy. But a goal clearly stated on paper is a serious commitment to yourself. As author Gary Ryan Blair says:

"Once a goal is written, you've made an investment. By choosing a goal and writing it down, you gain an edge. You execute best with precise instructions. Your written goal should be specific and measurable. What was once recorded on paper will soon be recorded in history…as a goal achieved."

Next, we are going to calculate how much money you would need to accumulate to pay you the amount needed to live your dream lifestyle.

I suggest you use the 7% withdrawal formula that my brother Paul and I featured in our first book: *The FAST TRACK to Financial Independence*.

Here is how the 7% withdrawal formula works:

Let's say that in the future you had the knowledge of how to return 20% each year. If you attained that knowledge, you could then safely draw down 7% to pay for your ideal lifestyle.

Let's do this working out together on a calculator.

Tap in the amount you said you would like each year and divide it by 7 and then multiply it by 100. This is the amount you would need to accumulate to give you the annual cash flow to create and live a dream lifestyle.

The capital mass amount needed to pay for your dream lifestyle is:

£_____

Next, when is your deadline?

Most of my clients say something in the region of 5-10 years.

Your deadline:_____

Finally, you need to work out your new capital mass. This is after inflation has been factored in. I normally use a figure of 3% per year.

The way to calculate this is simple. Take a look at this table below. You will notice that the maximum number of years to deadline is ten. I have done this because most people want to get to their goal in ten years or less and I am assuming that you are no different.

Number of Years to Your Deadline	Calculation to Use
1	+ 3%
2	+ 6.1%
3	+ 9.3%
4	+ 12.6%
5	+ 16%
6	+ 19.4%
7	+ 23%
8	+ 26.7%
9	+ 30.5%
10	+ 34.4%

To help, here are a couple of examples.

Example 1

Your goal is to make £5 million and your deadline is 5 years.

The calculation would be as follows:

5000000 + 16% =

The answer you get is £5.8 million.

Example 2

Your goal is to make £3 million in 7 years.

3000000 + 23% =

The answer you get is £3.69 million.

Now it is time to do your calculation. All you need is a standard calculator that has a % button.

Once you have worked out your new target with inflation factored in, simply write in the space below, your new capital mass figure.

Your new capital mass figure is £_____

This new capital mass figure now becomes your main aim and needs to be burned into your mind.

And to make sure what we have just done is crystal clear, here is an example of the full process.

Step 1 - When asked how much it would cost you to live one year of your dream lifestyle, you answer £70,000 (after tax).

Step 2 - The capital mass you would need to pay yourself £70,000 per year would be £1 million (£70,000 divided by 7 and multiplied by 100).

Step 3 - Because you want to get to your dream lifestyle in 10 years, you calculate that the amount you really need to accumulate is £1.34 million (with inflation factored in). You work this out using the previous, ten year table.

Step 4 - If you accumulated £1.34 million over the next ten years, you would then be able to pay yourself a 7% withdrawal each year, which would mean you could pay yourself £93,800 per year—and that £93,800 would give you the same purchasing power as £70,000 in today's terms.

Step 5 - Your £93,800 per year of cash flow would pay for a dream lifestyle. Plus, because you would have the knowledge of how to grow your wealth at 20% per year, you would not only get richer but your lifestyle would improve each and every year.

Step 6 - In this example, your £1.34 million would grow into £1.5 million (after deducting the 7% withdrawal to pay for your lifestyle, the remaining capital would grow at 20%) which would mean the following year you would have £105,000 to pay for one year of a dream lifestyle.

This means you just got richer and your dream lifestyle just got dreamier.

It is good to know that when you have accumulated enough money to allow you to live your dream lifestyle, you have reached a stage in your life where you can proudly say that you are Financially Free.

But how is that different from becoming Financially Independent?

In our first book, *The FAST TRACK to Financial Independence*, Paul and I explained that only 5% of the population make it to Financial Independence. We also stated that only 1% of the population become wealthy or Financially Free.[50] People have different interpretations of what these two terms mean. This is what they mean to us:

Financial Independence - *To have accumulated an amount of money so large that you are no longer influenced or controlled by others to sustain a "comfortable" lifestyle.*

Financial Freedom - *To have accumulated an amount of money so large that you are no longer influenced or controlled by others to sustain a "dream" lifestyle.*

To keep this nice and simple, Financial Independence equals a *comfortable* lifestyle and Financial Freedom equals *dream* or *ideal* lifestyle.

Therefore, Financial Independence is a stepping stone towards Financial Freedom.

Why So Many People Fail

The first point to note is this. Even though many people are living a comfortable lifestyle, it does not make them Financially Independent. Why? Because these same people pay for their comfortable lifestyle with money they earn from their boss or customers.

Therefore some people mistakenly think that they are Financially Independent. But by not understanding what Financial Independence really is, they set themselves up for potential future financial disaster.

If these same people decided to cash in their chips and sell all their assets, there is not a chance that they would generate enough money to allow them to live comfortably off the interest generated. It is therefore their boss or customers who dictate whether they get paid or not. In other words, their boss or customers have the *power*.

Financial Independence is when you are not reliant on anybody to live your comfortable lifestyle. It means that if the Financially Independent individual decided to cash in their chips from the sale of their assets, they would have enough money to allow them to live comfortably off the interest generated.

Being Wealthy Helps You to Choose What You Want to Do

Financial Independence gives *you* the power and not your boss or customers. The same goes for Financial Freedom; you have the power. Cornelius Vanderbilt, who was once the wealthiest man in the United States said, *"A million or two is as much as anyone ought to have, but what you have is not worth anything unless you have the power."*

You get that power when you have built up enough assets to allow you to be very choosy when it comes to whom you do business with. Let me give you a clear example of what I mean. When my brother Paul has time, he offers special one-to-one sessions with prospective clients. During these sessions, he takes them through a process that involves no selling, no jargon—just the facts. This time spent together helps both Paul and the prospective client determine if the premium service is suited to their needs.

These sessions are called Personal Consultations. They are valued at £1997 but sometimes as a special promotion, we offer them for free. The session consists of a one-to-one, highly personalised telephone conversation that generally lasts between one and two hours. They are purposefully designed to help you as the client get clear on whether or not we can help you.

Unfortunately for some people trying to book a session, Paul has to say no. Yes, they may have the money to pay for the premium service we offer, but unfortunately the answer is still no.

Why is this?

Because Paul and I are Financially Free, this freedom gives us the luxury to pick and choose who we want to do business with. And Paul has to be extra selective because the service we offer is soon going to be capped off; meaning we can only offer the "shadow" investing service to a limited number of people.

You see, because time is so precious, our goal is to spend it with people that we like. Life is simply too short to be spending it with people who don't sing from the same hymn sheet. We also want to work with clients for life. Our business is all about a relationship and not just a transaction. We look at things in terms of who do we want to help? To put it another way, Paul and I only want to help people that we get on with. Our team also share this philosophy and like us, will not put up with people who don't match our values.

This is an example of having the power to choose who you want to work, deal or do business with. And it is a truly great feeling. It's the feeling you get when you reach true Financial Independence. And the feeling gets even better as you approach Financial Freedom—which I'm assuming is your ultimate goal.

Can you imagine having that sort of power?

The power to say to your boss, "I am not coming in today because I have other things to do." Or, "I am sorry, Mr Prospect, but even though you want to purchase our product or service, I am afraid we can not help you."

Well I can assure you that you will one day have this power if you follow the system outlined in this book.

Would One Million Pounds in Liquid Make You Financially Free?

Earlier we talked about Financial Independence and Financial Freedom but where does the term Liquid Millionaire fit into this? Does it fit under the category of Financial Independence or Financial Freedom?

There is no straight answer to that question because both Financial Independence and Financial Freedom are different for every single person. But to help you understand where it slots in, let's imagine that magic million-pound figure. One million pounds liquid is a lot of money. Invested intelligently, one million pounds liquid could pay you £70,000 per year forever.

Would £70,000 (tax-free) give you a *comfortable* lifestyle?

If you answered yes, it tells you that hitting a million pounds worth of liquid capital would mean you were Financially Independent.

Would £70,000 per year enable you to experience and live a *dream* lifestyle?

If you answered yes, then one million pounds of liquid would make you Financially Free. So what sort of life could you create for yourself if you did become a liquid millionaire or even a liquid multi-millionaire?

What would your dream life look, sound and feel like?

To help you, I am going to talk about the type of ideal lifestyle this book can help you to create. Of course, your dream lifestyle may be totally different but at least you will get a few ideas about what is possible.

Becoming Liquid

First of all, when you have accumulated enough tax-free wealth to allow you to retire rich, it means that you are liquid. When you are liquid, it means you have substantial assets that can easily and quickly be converted into cash. This means that you can access money quickly should an emergency arise. Many property investors unfortunately do not have this luxury as most of their wealth is tied up in bricks and mortar.

As Gordon Gekko said in the 1987 blockbuster, *Wall Street*, *"I'm talking about liquid. Rich enough to have your own jet. Rich enough not to waste time. Fifty, a hundred million dollars, buddy. A player."*

How would it feel if you attained that much liquidity?

Create Your Own Quality World

Becoming a liquid millionaire or liquid multi-millionaire also allows you to create your very own Quality World. This might include living in a home that has been purposely designed just for you. You can, if you want, employ a team of people to make life easier (for example a housekeeper, gardener, nanny, cook, cleaner).

You are also able to pay cash for your dream car and have the financial means to enjoy it. Retiring rich also allows you to be able to go where you want to go at weekends and not worry about the cost.

You are also able to have plenty of holidays, including at least one once in a lifetime holiday per year. The quality world that you create is almost completely stress free and only includes the things that you want in it. The money you have allows you to choose to spend your time in situations of low stress and completely avoid situations of high stress. You are in complete control of what happens in your life and this feeling of being in control gives you a real sense of fulfilment, happiness and peace of mind.

You feel certain and confident about what direction your life is heading in. The money you have made allows your quality world to be a healthy, vibrant world. And when you live in a world with very little stress, it helps you to live a longer, healthier life which in turn helps you to enjoy your wealth and dream lifestyle for even longer.

By using your wealth to focus on your well-being, it helps you remain strong, healthy, pain free, independent, fit and full of energy. Living in a quality world allows you to have the ability to spend time fostering deep, loving relationships with your family and friends and sharing magic moments with them.

How would it feel to have enough cash to create your very own quality world?

Money Is No Longer a Worry

Because money is no longer a worry, you realise that time is now your most precious commodity and that you only have one shot at life. You remind yourself that there are no action replays. You therefore carefully plan to make each and every day a success. You make a decision to spend your time on things of pleasure, things that bring joy and happiness to your life. You avoid as much as possible things that cause pain, unhappiness or misery.

Attaining liquid millionaire or liquid multi-millionaire status can also help you to have and enjoy peace of mind over all money matters.

You feel financially secure, removing all previous money worries. When you have built up seven or even eight figures of tax-free income, it would probably mean that you could retire right away if you wanted to.

How would you feel if you had complete peace of mind over all money matters and were in a position to retire?

Having Enough Money Equals Freedom

Bestselling author and entrepreneur Michael Masterson once said, *"The most valuable thing that money can buy is the freedom to spend your time as you see fit."*

And I agree, because when you are a liquid millionaire, you feel free. It helps to give you a feeling of full control over your life. You have no boss or significant other telling you what you can or can't do.

And as I mentioned before, if you have a business, your financial position allows you to have the power to choose who you want to do business with. Being free gives you the option of getting up late if you want to.

What a luxury.

Plus, if you want to take a last-minute break in Monte Carlo, Paris or Milan, you can do it.

Or if you decided one day that you wanted to clock off at lunch, you can do that too. Becoming liquid rich helps to get rid of all your consumer debt.

Having that much cash would mean you would never need to borrow money to buy things that decrease in value over time. You would be able to have zero debt on things such as credit cards and personal loans.

Being Able to Leave Your Mark

Plus…having that much capital gives you the option to share your wealth. You could do things for the greater good. You might want to use your wealth to make the planet a better place. You might plan to leave a legacy or become a philanthropist like Bill Gates, Warren Buffett, Sir Tom Hunter or Andrew Carnegie.

Imagine having the option of being able to give all that cash away in the second half of your life.

Does that sort of thinking get you going?

The possibilities are endless.

Make Your Life a Masterpiece

In summary then, becoming a liquid millionaire or liquid multi-millionaire allows you to experience life to the full. It can help you turn your life into a masterpiece. You have the power to make it into anything that you want. And when you create a masterpiece with your life, you really enjoy your existence to the max. You adore the life experience and this is clearly highlighted in your daily interactions with others. The money allows you to squeeze every bit of juice out of life. You take in as many experiences as possible. You go to see things. You go and do things. You live and enjoy experience after experience after experience.

It really is amazing what being rich can do for you.

Visualise Your Goal

Before we move on, I have some final words about creating your dream lifestyle. If you have heard or read about the power of visualisation, you will know that by seeing your goal as completed in your mind's eye and fully engaging all your senses (see, hear, touch, taste and smell), your goal will become your reality much sooner.

As Michelangelo once famously said, *"I saw the angel in the marble and carved until I set him free."*

And as Brian Tracy says: *"Your visual images become your reality. They intensify your desires and deepen your beliefs. They increase your willpower and build your persistence. They are enormously powerful."*

Stephen Sutherland (left), Brian Tracy (centre) and
Paul Sutherland (right) in London.

There are four elements of visualisation[51] and an increase in any one of them will accelerate the rate at which you create the physical equivalent of that mental picture in your life.

The four elements are:

1. *Frequency*: How often you visualise.

2. *Vividness*: How much clarity your pictures have when you visualise.

3. *Intensity*: The amount of emotion you combine with your visualisations.

4. *Duration*: The length of time you can hold the picture in your mind.

If you are really serious about retiring rich, I suggest that you aim to carry out visualisation exercises—where you focus on your dream lifestyle—every single day. In fact, thinking about what it is that you want and how you plan to get it should be on your mind during as much of the waking day as possible.

If you want it badly enough, this will happen automatically.

But to get things going, first thing in the morning and last thing at night are ideal for visualisation exercises. Imagining your goal as real and already accomplished is extremely powerful and is yet another way to help you maximize your probability of success.

As George Bernard Shaw once wrote, *"Imagination is the beginning of creation. You imagine what you desire, you will what you imagine and at last you create what you will."*

Now we can quickly move on to discovering exactly how to make the money needed to create this lifestyle for you.

Are you ready?

Are you sure?

Great.

But before that, let's discuss the speed at which you will get there. For example, when my brother Paul is on the phone to a potential client, they sometimes say to him…

"Paul, if I am going to spend thousands of pounds[52] to shadow invest Stephen, what sort of returns will I make, say over the first 12-24 months?"

Want to know how he answers that question?

Good, because you are now going to find out …

CHAPTER 3

A Sure-Fire Way to Know How Much Money You Are Likely to Make in <u>ANY</u> Given Period of Time

---

"Historically, three out of four stocks have followed the general market trend–up as well as down."
- William O'Neil

There is a very useful tool that I created and I think you will like it. This tool can help you to quickly determine how much money you will make in any given period of time. Its name is *The Performance Quadrant*.

The performance quadrant is unique.

How much profit you will make in any length of time, whether it is twelve months, two years or a decade will ALWAYS depend on **four factors**. By discovering how the performance quadrant works, you will realise that when making money in the stock market, there are some things that are in your control and others that aren't. Let me explain:-

What's in Your Control and What Isn't?

In the last chapter, I mentioned a question that many potential clients ask my brother Paul;

"If I am going to spend thousands of pounds to shadow invest Stephen, what sort of returns will I make, say over the first 12-24 months?"

Paul always replies with …"I have no idea."

Then he quickly explains…

"What I can say, however, is that my main aim is to help you make greater than average tax-free returns over the long-term. And when I say greater than average tax-free returns, I am talking about something in the region of between 15% and 20% over the long run."

Then he moves on to explaining how the performance quadrant works.

So what would you like first—the good news or the bad news?

The good news is that two of the components making up the performance quadrant are in your control. The bad news is that two of the components are totally and utterly out of your control. To put it another way, it is literally impossible to predict how much money you are likely to make, especially in a short period of time such as one or two years. In longer periods, it becomes easier to predict and you will learn why as you make your way through this book.

Let's now talk about each part of the performance quadrant because all four determine in some way how much cash you will make.

The Two Parts of the Performance Quadrant *in* Your Control

The first part in the quadrant is the investment and by this I mean the Investment Vehicle.

THE PERFORMANCE QUADRANT

INTERNAL (in your control)	EXTERNAL (out of your control)
INVESTMENT VEHICLE	MARKET DIRECTION
MARKET TIMING	MARKET STRENGTH

Investment Vehicle

This relates to which investment vehicle or vehicles you choose to buy throughout your investing career. To begin, you need to decide on which type of investment you are going to use. Because there are so many different types of investment vehicles to choose from, trying to become an expert in each one is going to take more time than you have available.

Would you like to know what my personal choice is?

The answer is something called *Investment Funds*. You may know investment funds by the names Unit Trusts or Open Ended Investment Companies or OEICS's (pronounced oiks). And so the first thing that is in your control is your choice of investment vehicle. Later I am going to be showing you how I made it possible to search through the thousands of funds out there and find the very best ones.[53]

For example, through my investment fund screening tool (HIRE CAR™)–which helps you to find the best of the best investment funds–it found and helped us to invest in the Number 1 performing investment fund of 2003. It was called the Framlington Japan Fund (now called the AXA Framlington Japan Fund) and in that one single year, it made a return of 91.05%. Yes, HIRE CAR™ found it and we invested all our ISA money into it.

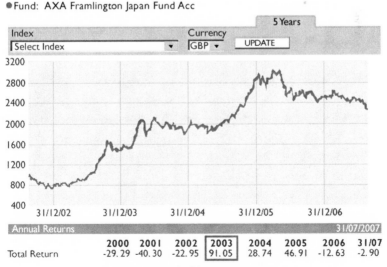

● Fund: AXA Framlington Japan Fund Acc

	2000	2001	2002	2003	2004	2005	2006	31/07
Total Return	-29.29	-40.30	-22.95	91.05	28.74	46.91	-12.63	-2.90

Data Supplied by Morningstar.

Market Timing

The second part in the performance quadrant—that will determine how much money you will make in any given period of time is timing. And when I say timing, I mean market timing. This, like finding the best investment funds to invest into, is also in your control. This is about getting into the market when the market is in an uptrend and getting out of the market when the uptrend changes into a downtrend.

When you get in, you get into the fund that you have carefully selected and when you get out, you <u>switch</u> into the safety of a cash based investment.

There is a very good reason for switching into cash when the market shows clear signs of weakness (downtrend) and this will be fully explained as we move through the book. With switching in and out of the market at the most opportune times, it allows you to make money on strength (uptrend) and you protect your money when the market is weak and trending down.

You will learn exactly how and why we do this switching in and switching out of the market a little later.

Timing Is Crucial to Your Success

Why is getting the timing right so crucial?

What I have found is that the investment strategy of buy and hold does not work. Instead, to win, you need to be active. Anyone who used a buy and hold strategy and bought (as many did) just before the 2000-2002 savage bear (down) market, will have been nursing potential losses of up to 90% on their portfolios. Dropping 90% means your portfolio has to then make 900% just to get back even.

How long would that take?

Buy and hold therefore carries too much risk.

This second key part in the performance quadrant tells you that even if you pick the very best investment vehicle, if you get your timing wrong, your overall performance will be severely affected.

The Two Parts of the Performance Quadrant *out* of Your Control

Now you have seen what is in your control, let's take a look more closely at the two things that are out of your control. Here is the quadrant again to remind you:

THE PERFORMANCE QUADRANT

INTERNAL (in your control)	EXTERNAL (out of your control)
INVESTMENT VEHICLE	MARKET DIRECTION
MARKET TIMING	MARKET STRENGTH

Direction

The third part of the performance quadrant that will determine how much money you will make in any given period of time is direction. When I say direction I mean market direction. In Chapter 5, you discover a key fundamental fact about how the stock market really works. But here is a quick taster:

Three out of every four stocks (and investment funds) move in the same direction as the market.

That tells you that **the performance of the funds you choose throughout your investing career will be directly linked to the market's direction.** If the market is trending up, three out of every four funds will move up. And that means if the market is trending down, funds are going to move down.

And if the market is trending sideways they are going to move in which direction?

Yes, you are correct–sideways.

Collectively, this indicates that if a client decided to sign up for a multi year shadow investing package[54]–and the market over the next 12-24 months went down or sideways–how much money is this person likely to make?

If you said nothing or very little, you would be right on the money. And this is just one of the things that are pointed out to the potential client when contemplating coming on board. I always explain that the system we use to make these greater than average tax-free returns needs patience.

Why Cursing the Market Gets You Nowhere

It is impossible to will the market upwards. And if it does not go up, funds are not going to go up either. But the good news is that, as you saw on the chart in the introduction, since the stock markets began in

1893 the general trend of the market is up and that means that if you are patient, sooner or later the market will move up and that is when there is always some big money to be made. The market can therefore do one of three things. It can either trend up, down or sideways. The key question that you need to be constantly asking yourself is this:

Which way is the stock market heading? Is it trending up, down or sideways?

Market Strength

The fourth and final part that determines how much money you will make in any given period of time is market strength.

THE PERFORMANCE QUADRANT

INTERNAL
(in your control)

EXTERNAL
(out of your control)

INVESTMENT VEHICLE

MARKET DIRECTION

MARKET TIMING

MARKET STRENGTH

If the market's uptrend is strong, funds are also going to be strong. For example in 1999, the Nasdaq went up 86% in one year and this was its best year's performance in its entire history.[55] In that very same year, investment funds were moving up 100%, 200%, 300% and even 400% in just one year.[56]

Why?

Well, if you have started to put the investment puzzle together, you will have realised that <u>funds were making huge gains because the market was also making huge gains</u>. In other words, it was in an extremely strong uptrend. If we move to another year and compare 1999 with 2003, you will start to see the reason why market strength plays an essential role in determining how much money you are likely to make in any given period of time.

You see, in 2003 the Nasdaq went up 50%.[57] This is still classed as a good year but it was clearly not as strong as 1999 when it went up 86%. In 2003, the top performing fund was a fund I mentioned earlier, the AXA Framlington Japan Fund. It went up 91.05% which is a great return but it was clearly not as strong as the best performing funds back in 1999.

The All Important Link

Can you now see the link between the fund you buy, the market direction and the market's strength?

Good.

Can you also see that timing your buying will also play an essential role in how much money you make?

I am assuming at this point that you are starting to see the all important connection between the four parts that make up the performance quadrant. Because you are still reading this, it tells me that you are probably a person who is prepared to be patient when the market is heading sideways or downwards. That is a good sign.

Now here is a great question.

What is the probability that you will need to be patient over the next few years?

I believe very low and this is where it starts to get very exciting.

The Market Looks as if It's Due a Move

One of the things my clients and I are thrilled about right now is this fact:

The market has not moved very much over the last 10 years and when a market moves sideways for a long period of time, sooner or later it MUST continue its upward trend.[58] And when it does continue this uptrend you have a much higher probability of making money because three out of every four stocks and funds move in the same direction as the market.

Let me remind you of an example we looked at earlier. We all know that over the last decade, property prices have shot up significantly.[59] But let's imagine that property prices had actually moved sideways over the last ten years. Let's continue to imagine that property values had not made any price progress over the last decade, meaning you could now buy property at the same price they were ten years ago.

If you could buy property at prices they were a decade ago, would that provide you with an appealing investment opportunity?

The answer is, of course.

Would it guarantee that you would make money in property?

The answer is no, but if we go back to the concept of probability, the probability would be high.

Still not convinced?

Take a look at this chart of the UK property market. Notice the ten year period highlighted between 1985 and 1995.

Can you see that house prices did not move over that ten year period?

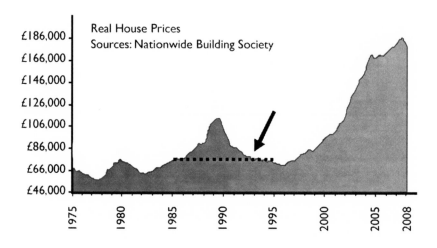

Source: www.HousePriceCrash.co.uk

In other words, this chart clearly shows that in 1995, you could buy houses at 1985's prices. Now I want you to imagine that a successful property market investor had shown you this chart back in 1995 and explained to you that house prices were probably due a move over the next ten years.

Would this inside information have got you to say, "I want in"?

If in reality this had happened to you and you acted, it is obvious that you could have made yourself a small fortune.

Award-winning poet and author Robin Morgan once famously wrote, *"Knowledge is power. Information is power."*

And I would like to add; "......But only when acted upon."

Nobody Wants a Life Filled with Regret

Bestselling author Richard Carlson once wrote, "*The old adage, 'If it sounds too good to be true, it probably is,' isn't always correct. In fact, the suspicion, cynicism and doubt that are inherent in this belief can and does keep people from taking advantage of excellent opportunities.*"

You see, if we miss a wonderful opportunity to help us retire rich, we then face the possibility of a life filled with regret. In fact, we may even end up hating ourselves if we do nothing when we know we should.

Now here is something that we discussed earlier that might once again get you sitting up in your chair.

Stock markets' and property markets' trends over the long-term are up. And from time to time they have to correct in price, rest, recuperate and then start to gather strength for their next run. In other words, when the property or stock market moves sideways in price over a long period of time, sooner or later it has to resume its upwards trend.

And as you keep hearing, the stock market over the last 10 years has hardly moved in price.

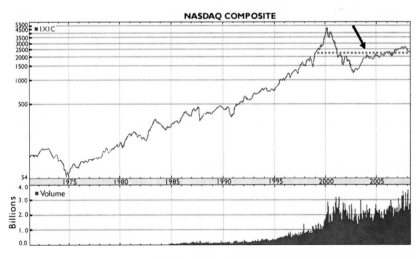

Data Supplied by Yahoo.

Just like in the property price chart you saw earlier, in the last 10 years, the stock market's gone up and it has come down. And as you can see on this chart, when you draw a trend line between the price it was at in 1998 and the price it was at the end of 2007, you can see that it has literally drifted sideways, making hardly any price progress.

With the stock market, history tends to repeat itself. This is very good news for you, especially when you are armed with some key historical data. You have seen an example of the property market making no price progress for a ten year period and then exploding northwards.

But what about the stock market? Has the stock market done this before?

Yes.

From 1970 to 1980 the stock market hardly made any price progress.[60]

Do you know what happened after that 1970-1980 ten year period?

If you don't, take a look at this chart to see what happened.

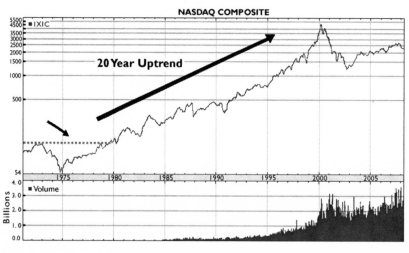

Data Supplied by Yahoo.

As you can see, it went on a 20 year run. And if it goes on a similar run over the next ten to twenty years, what is going to happen to your portfolio? You don't have to be a rocket scientist to work that one out.

Let's summarise what we have learned so far.

If you have a reliable and consistent system of finding the best funds, buying them when the market is strong and healthy, moving out onto the sidelines when the market weakens and the market does have a strong upwards move over the next 10-20 years, you, my friend could hit the jackpot.

Nasdaq 76,430

The Nasdaq market at the end of 2007 closed at 2652. If the market does what it did in the past, at the end of 2027, the Nasdaq is going to be trading at 76,430.[61] That's more than a 2780% move.

But before we get too far ahead of ourselves, let's focus in on the next 10 years. And what sort of returns can you expect if the market does make a strong move over the next 10 years? I reckon that with some fancy fund picking and a touch of luck, you could make close to 30% annualised returns.

Really?

Yes, really.

... but that would only be possible in a very strong market environment.

However, if the decade of 1990-2000 was replicated (which I believe is highly probable) where we saw the Nasdaq go up on average 24.5% per year and if you have a system of being able to beat the Nasdaq, 30% returns might just be achievable. But what is achievable for people who have generally no idea what they are doing and rely on a financial adviser, stock broker or their local bank manager?

Learn–and Your Wealth Increases

Well, most of the people we speak to us they have the knowledge, skill and confidence to return about 6% per year over the next ten years. And this is when Paul helps the client calculate what they are likely to make in tax-free income over the next ten years with their current skills, knowledge and contacts. After seeing how 6% growth rates affect the client's capital over various periods of time, Paul proceeds to show them what their money would turn into if they could get it to grow at greater than average returns.

When they discover the difference, Paul tells me that they are literally speechless.

Would you be interested in finding out these figures that Paul discusses with our clients?

Would you also like to know what he tells the client–when he shows them how it might just be possible to make millions of pounds in tax-free income– in the up and coming stock market boom–if you know what you are doing?

Fantastic. Because you are about to find out ...

CHAPTER 4

A Way to Make Up to 30% Returns over the Next 10 Years

"The stock market is the world's biggest goldmine."
– Jesse Livermore

As I said in the last chapter, most people simply do not have the skill or knowledge to make greater than average tax-free returns.

Why?

Part of the answer is that they have never been taught.

Because the majority of people do not *believe* it is possible to achieve 15%, 20%, 30% or even higher returns by skilfully investing in the stock market, they never get off the starting blocks.

Bestselling author Dr. David Schwartz has this to say on the power of belief. *"Believe it can be done. When you believe something can be done, really believe, your mind will find the ways to do it."*

You see, because people do not believe it's possible to make big returns in the stock market, any time they hear somebody claim it's possible, they either say that the person is a fraud or a rare genius.

Don't Shoot Yourself in the Foot

In other words; they shoot themselves in the foot before even starting.

I used to think that returning more than 7% on your money was impossible.

That was before I became educated in the stock market. But now I am certain that it is possible to beat the market because not only have I done it but there are countless other investors who have done it too.

So if you want to know how to make big percentage gains over the next five to ten years, where should you start to look?

Who has the answers?

Who can help you learn what you need to learn to succeed in the stock market?

Learn the how to from those who are already succeeding. Find people with great track records. Find experts in the field you need help with. Don't go for theory people. Go for people with superb results.

Can it be that simple?

Yes.

At the end of the last chapter we talked about the sort of gains that would be possible for people who have no idea what they are doing. I also mentioned that most clients that my brother Paul speaks to tell him that they have the knowledge needed to return about 6% per year over the next ten years. So with that, we are now going to look at what happens to money when it grows at low rates of return compared to higher rates of return.

Make Millions in Tax-Free Income

I am also going to show you how it is possible (if you know what you are doing) to make millions in tax-free income.[62]

In this chapter, we will focus on some numbers, or the theory of what happens to money over time when grown at different rates of return. I will show you how your money would grow if it was returning small rates of percentage growth and also what impact larger rates of return would have.

And in the next chapter, I am going to share with you how it's possible to turn the theory of greater than average tax-free returns into reality.

Are you familiar with the term *compounding?*

I am assuming you are.

If you are not, all you need to know for now is that money will grow into different amounts over time depending on what rate of return you can get it to grow at.

The rule is, the higher the rate of return, the more your money grows.

But generally, the higher the rate of return, the more risk that comes with it. But you can *reduce* that risk in two ways. You can lower risk by becoming educated in how the market works. You can also reduce risk by switching out of the market when it's unhealthy.

Now we are going to use three examples to illustrate how money can grow over different time periods and at different rates of return.

The three case studies below are based on the financial picture of my typical clients—so hopefully one of them will be similar to your current situation.

Case Study 1	Case Study 2	Case Study 3
Married 35 Years old.	Married 45 Years old.	Married 50 Years old.
High Income.	High Income.	High Income.
Tax-Free Savings: No.	Tax-Free Savings: £250,000	Tax-Free Savings: £650,000

First of all notice that they are all earning high incomes.[63]

What does this mean? It tells you that they could (if they wanted to) afford to put in the full ISA allowance of £14,400 each and every year.

But please note that some of my more mature clients, who are already retired, are no longer earning large incomes—but this does not rule them out.

I do not exclude them because over their working years, they have built up a substantial amount of liquid capital (normally £100,000 plus) which means they can simply grow their cash lump sum and still get to their goal without having to also invest on a monthly or yearly basis, as some of my younger clients do.

Getting back to the case studies, notice that as each client gains age, their Tax-Free Savings pot tends to rise. In other words, I find that the majority of my clients aged 50 upwards have large pension and ISA portfolios and with many of them being business owners, their pension is either in a SIPP already or they have the ability to turn it into one if they want to.

It is good to know that all personal and private pensions can be turned into a SIPP.

And just so that you are aware, when a person is an employee of a company, and has a company pension, this type of pension can't be turned into a SIPP.

That is why most people who take out a SIPP are either self-employed professionals or business owners. The only exception to this rule are people who have deferred or frozen pensions—ones that have been built up from previous employers—as these can also be turned into a SIPP.

If you are unsure, speak to your adviser and ask them to explain in plain English what a SIPP is and how they work.

Moving on, before we look at some projections, to simplify things, we named the combination of my clients' ISA and SIPP money, Tax-Free Savings.

For example, in case study three their tax-free savings are £650,000. This £650,000 could have been made up from say £500,000 in a pension and £150,000 in ISAs.

It is now time to show you how your money would grow if it was returning small rates of percentage growth and also what impact larger rates of return would have on it.

Let's start with case study number one.

We will begin with taking a look at what happens to each couple's finances if they were growing their wealth at 6% per year over the next 10 years.

Then we will move on to how their wealth grows if they could get their cash to grow at 30% per year.

And finally, we will look at what sort of amount of wealth they could accumulate by the time they reach the standard retirement age of 65.

We will then move on to case study two and do exactly the same thing.

We will complete the illustration with case study number three. When you have looked at all three case studies, I think you might be surprised by the huge difference knowledge can make in the overall level of wealth you can create over various time frames.

We will be using a special Tax-Free Savings Compounding Calculator to work out these amounts.

The calculator used for these up and coming examples is one that our clients get free access to.

But we are not the only company to have such calculators. If you want to have a play with some figures, do a search on Google. Your goal should be to find a calculator that does two things.

1. Calculates what growth you get on your money over time, when grown at different rates of return, when **adding to your pot monthly or annually**.

2. Calculates what growth you get on your money over time, when grown at different rates of return, when starting with a **lump sum**.

Case Study 1

Case Study 1
Married 35 Years old.
High Income.
Tax-Free Savings: No

Investing £14,400 per Year at 6% Growth over 10 Years

This couple are starting with zero in tax-free savings.

But because the couple are receiving a high household income, they have the ability to invest £14,400 per year into their ISA which equates to £1200 per month.

To do our calculation, we simply tap into the Monthly Savings Plan Calculator the following figures.

In the Monthly Payment box, we type in 1200 representing £1200.

In the Duration box, we type in 10 and in the Interest Rate (annually) box, we type in 6.

When we hit calculate, the calculator quickly works out how much the saved £1200 per month would grow into if grown at 6% over the next 10 years.

Here is the result:

Monthly Savings Plan

Find out how much a regular monthly savings scheme could make.

Monthly Payment   £ | 1200

Duration | 10 | **Years**

Interest Rate (annually) | 6 | **%**

RESULT   Calculate **>>**

Your investment will be worth*   £ | 197,638.49

*This calculator assumes an initial balance of zero and that savings are made for a full month before interest is calculated and compounded.

As you can see, the net result is one hundred and ninety seven thousand, six hundred and thirty eight pounds and forty nine pence.

Growing money at 6% does not usually appeal to my clients after they realise that with the right knowledge, it is possible to grow money at much higher returns.

As you will soon see, it might be possible to make as much as 30% annual returns over the next 10 years, if you know what you are doing.[64]

As billionaire businessman Sir Richard Branson once wrote, *"I firmly believe that anything is possible."*

Let's take a look at case study number one but this time with higher growth projections.

Investing £14,400 per Year at 30% Growth over 10 Years

To do our calculation, we simply tap into the Monthly Savings Plan Calculator the following figures.

In the Monthly Payment box, we type in 1200 representing £1200.

In the Duration box, we type in 10 and in the Interest Rate (annually) box, we type in 30.

When we hit calculate the calculator quickly works out how much the saved £1200 per month would grow into if grown at 30% over the next 10 years. Here is the result:

Monthly Savings Plan

Find out how much a regular monthly savings scheme could make.

Monthly Payment	£ 1200
Duration	10 Years
Interest Rate (annually)	30 %
RESULT	Calculate >>
Your investment will be worth*	£ 903,220.97

*This calculator assumes an initial balance of zero and that savings are made for a full month before interest is calculated and compounded.

As you can see, the net result is nine hundred and three thousand, two hundred and twenty pounds and ninety seven pence.

Now let's compare the 6% returns versus the 30% returns. Remember that in both cases, the only difference is the annual rate of growth.

Case Study 1	Investing Amounts	Number of Years Investing	At 6% Growth	At 30% Growth
Married 35 Years old. High Income. Tax-Free Savings: No.	£14,400 per Year	10 Years	£198,000	£903,000

Now let's extend the 10 year period to see what kinds of money could be made by the time this couple gets to age 65. Because this couple are aged 35, we can do our projections on 30 years growth. These next projections are based on the 35 year old couple continuing to add the full ISA allowance of £14,400 each and every year.

But I have to warn you that returning up to 30% over long periods of time is not going to be easy. In fact it is going to be very difficult ... but it may be possible.

As billionaire retailer Sam Walton once said, *"High expectations are the key to everything."*

Aiming to get 30% returns for a period of longer than 10 years is going to be much more difficult—even if the market does move up powerfully.

With this in mind, in the projections you are about to see, I have used a 30 year long-term growth target of 17.5% which is my best estimation of what is achievable over that length of time span.

Investing £14,400 per Year at 17.5% Growth over 30 Years

To do our calculation, we simply tap into the Monthly Savings Plan Calculator the following figures.

In the Monthly Payment box, we type in 1200 representing £1200.

In the Duration box, we type in 30 and in the interest rate (annually) box, we type in 17.5.

When we hit calculate, the calculator quickly works out how much the saved £1200 per month would grow into if grown at 17.5% over the next 30 years. Here is the result:

Monthly Savings Plan

Find out how much a regular monthly savings scheme could make.

Monthly Payment £ 1200

Duration 30 **Years**

Interest Rate (annually) 17.5 %

RESULT Calculate >>

Your investment will be worth* £ 15,234,185.71

*This calculator assumes an initial balance of zero and that savings are made for a full month before interest is calculated and compounded.

As you can see on the compounding calculator, the net result is a juicy fifteen million, two hundred and thirty four thousand, one hundred and eighty five pounds and seventy one pence.

Before we move onto the next case study, let's summarise what we have just learned.

Case Study 1 - Summary

Case Study 1

Married 35 Years old.

High Income.

Tax-Free Savings: No

Capital Invested	Projected Growth Rate	Length of Time Money Is Invested	Total Amount Money Grows Into
£14,400 per Year	6%	10 Years	£198,000
£14,400 per Year	30%	10 Years	£903,000
£14,400 per Year	17.5%	30 Years	£15.2 Million

If you have not been exposed to compounding before, you may be shocked by these differences. The first time I was introduced to compounding, I had trouble sleeping…for a long time.

Let's now move on to case study number two.

Case Study 2

Case Study 2
Married 45 Years old.
High Income.
Tax-Free Savings: £250,000

In case studies two and three, I have used not one but two compounding calculators.

The reason is because we have to look at the growth on <u>the money that they invest monthly</u> and the overall growth on their <u>tax-free lump sum</u>.

And as you will soon see, the two separate calculators cleverly calculate the total amount that the couple's money will grow into.

Notice that the couple in this example are not only able to save and invest £1200 per month, but they also have the advantage of already having a £250,000 tax-free savings lump sum.

Therefore the two calculators we will use to work out the answer are a Monthly Savings Plan Calculator and a Lump Sum Investments Calculator.

Just so that it's nice and clear, The Monthly Savings Plan Calculator will work out what their £1200 will grow into at different growth rates over various time periods and the Lump Sum Investments Calculator will work out what their £250,000 in tax-free savings will grow into—once again using different growth rates over various time periods.

This means that as well as getting their monthly investing amounts to grow, they can also get their lump sum of £250,000 growing too.

And to make things crystal, you will also see the total amount of money they could make by combining monthly saving and investing plus lump sum investing.

Investing £14,400 per Year at 6% + £250,000 Lump Sum at 6% (Growth over 10 Years)

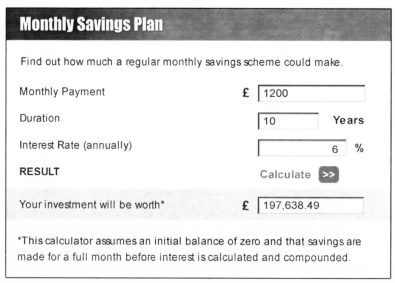

Or Lump Sum Investments

Calculate how much a lump sum investment could be worth.

Amount Invested   £ | 250,000

Duration | 10 | **Years**

Interest Rate (annually) | 6 | %

RESULT   Calculate **>>**

Your investment will be worth*   £ | 447,711.92

*This calculator assumes an initial balance of zero and that savings are made for a full year before interest is calculated and compounded.

Grand Total (Monthly and Lump Sum)

Your total investments will be worth   £ | 645,350.41

As you can see, the Grand Total result of their efforts would be six hundred and forty five thousand, three hundred and fifty pounds and forty one pence.

As I said before, growing money at 6% does not usually appeal to my clients after they realise that with the right knowledge, it is possible to grow it at much higher returns.

Let's take a look at what this case study looks like but with higher growth projections.

Investing £14,400 per Year at 30% + £250,000 Lump Sum at 30% (Growth over 10 Years)

Monthly Savings Plan

Find out how much a regular monthly savings scheme could make.

Monthly Payment   £ | 1200 |

Duration | 10 | **Years**

Interest Rate (annually) | 30 | %

RESULT   Calculate >>

Your investment will be worth*   £ | 903,220.97 |

*This calculator assumes an initial balance of zero and that savings are made for a full month before interest is calculated and compounded.

Or Lump Sum Investments

Calculate how much a lump sum investment could be worth.

Amount Invested   £ | 250,000 |

Duration | 10 | **Years**

Interest Rate (annually) | 30 | %

RESULT   Calculate >>

Your investment will be worth*   £ | 3,446,462.30 |

*This calculator assumes an initial balance of zero and that savings are made for a full year before interest is calculated and compounded.

Grand Total (Monthly and Lump Sum)

Your total investments will be worth   £ | 4,349,683.20 |

Now that is much better, isn't it?

As you can see on the compounding calculator, the net result is four million, three hundred and forty nine thousand, six hundred and eighty three pounds and twenty pence.

Now let's compare the 6% returns versus the +30% returns. Remember that in both cases, the only difference is the annual rate of growth.

Case Study 2	Investing Amounts	Number of Years Investing	At 6% Growth	At 30% Growth
Married 45 Years old. High Income. Tax-Free Savings: £250,000	£14,400 per Year + Lump Sum of £250,000	10 Years	£645,000	£4.3 Million

We can once again extend the 10 year period to see what kinds of money could be made by the time this couple gets to age 65. Because this couple are aged 45, we can do our projections on 20 years' growth. These next projections are based on this 45 year old couple adding their full ISA allowance of £14,400 each and every year for a 20 year period and also growing their lump sum of £250,000 over that same 20 year period.

As I stated last time, aiming to get 30% returns for a period of longer than 10 years is going to be much more difficult—even if the market does move up powerfully.

With this in mind, in the projections you are about to see, I have used a 20 year long-term growth target of 20% which is once again my best estimation of what is achievable over that length of time span.

Investing £14,400 per Year at 20% + £250,000 Lump Sum at 20% (Growth over 20 Years)

When we hit calculate, the calculator quickly works out how much the saved £1200 per month would grow into if grown at 20% over the next

20 years and what the £250,000 lump sum would grow into if this was also grown at 20% over the next 20 years.

Here is the result:

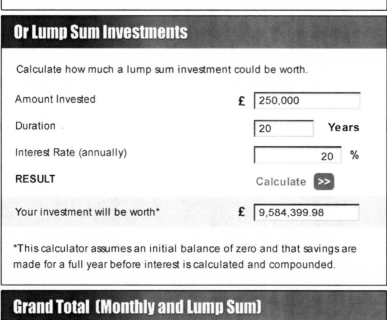

Monthly Savings Plan

Find out how much a regular monthly savings scheme could make.

Monthly Payment	£ 1200
Duration	20 **Years**
Interest Rate (annually)	20 %
RESULT	Calculate >>
Your investment will be worth*	£ 3,793,775.24

*This calculator assumes an initial balance of zero and that savings are made for a full month before interest is calculated and compounded.

Or Lump Sum Investments

Calculate how much a lump sum investment could be worth.

Amount Invested	£ 250,000
Duration	20 **Years**
Interest Rate (annually)	20 %
RESULT	Calculate >>
Your investment will be worth*	£ 9,584,399.98

*This calculator assumes an initial balance of zero and that savings are made for a full year before interest is calculated and compounded.

Grand Total (Monthly and Lump Sum)

Your total investments will be worth	£ 13,378,174.22

As you can see, the net result is a sizeable thirteen million, three hundred and seventy eight thousand, one hundred and seventy four pounds and twenty two pence.

Before we move onto the third and final case study, let's once again summarise what we have just learned.

Case Study 2 - Summary

Case Study 2
Married 45 Years old.
High Income.
Tax-Free Savings: £250,000

Capital Invested	Projected Growth Rate	Length of Time Money Is Invested	Total Amount Money Grows Into
£14,400 per Year + Lump Sum of £250,000	6%	10 Years	£645,000
£14,400 per Year + Lump Sum of £250,000	30%	10 Years	£4.3 Million
£14,400 per Year + Lump Sum of £250,000	20%	20 Years	£13.4 Million

Finally, let's now move on to case study number three.

Case Study 3

Case Study 3
Married 50 Years old.
High Income.
Tax-Free Savings: £650,000

In this third and final case study, I have once again used the two calculators which together will calculate the total amount that the couple's money will grow into.

As in case study number two, this couple are not only able to save and invest £1200 per month, but also have the advantage of already having a lump sum of tax-free savings.

In this case they have a starting sum of £650,000.

Therefore once again we need to use a Monthly Savings Plan Calculator and a Lump Sum Investments Calculator.

This means that as well as getting their £1200 per month to grow, they can also get their lump sum of £650,000 growing too.

And once again, to make things easier, you will also see the total amount.

Investing £14,400 per Year at 6% + £650,000 Lump Sum at 6% (Growth over 10 Years)

Monthly Savings Plan

Find out how much a regular monthly savings scheme could make.

Monthly Payment	£	1200
Duration		10 **Years**
Interest Rate (annually)		6 **%**
RESULT		Calculate **>>**
Your investment will be worth*	£	197,638.49

*This calculator assumes an initial balance of zero and that savings are made for a full month before interest is calculated and compounded.

Or Lump Sum Investments

Calculate how much a lump sum investment could be worth.

Amount Invested	£	650,000
Duration		10 **Years**
Interest Rate (annually)		6 **%**
RESULT		Calculate **>>**
Your investment will be worth*	£	1,164,051.00

*This calculator assumes an initial balance of zero and that savings are made for a full year before interest is calculated and compounded.

Grand Total (Monthly and Lump Sum)

Your total investments will be worth	£	1,361,689.49

The result is one million, three hundred and sixty one thousand, six hundred and eighty nine pounds and forty nine pence. Let's take a look at case study number three but this time with higher growth projections.

Investing £14,400 per Year at 30% + £650,000 Lump Sum at 30% (Growth over 10 Years)

Monthly Savings Plan

Find out how much a regular monthly savings scheme could make.

Monthly Payment	£ 1200
Duration	10 Years
Interest Rate (annually)	30 %
RESULT	Calculate >>
Your investment will be worth*	£ 903,220.97

*This calculator assumes an initial balance of zero and that savings are made for a full month before interest is calculated and compounded.

Or Lump Sum Investments

Calculate how much a lump sum investment could be worth.

Amount Invested	£ 650,000
Duration	10 Years
Interest Rate (annually)	30 %
RESULT	Calculate >>
Your investment will be worth*	£ 8,960,801.97

*This calculator assumes an initial balance of zero and that savings are made for a full year before interest is calculated and compounded.

Grand Total (Monthly and Lump Sum)

Your total investments will be worth	£ 9,864,028.94

As you can see on the compounding calculator, the net result is a tidy nine million, eight hundred and sixty four thousand, twenty eight pounds and ninety four pence.

Now let's once again compare the 6% returns versus the 30% returns. Remember that in both cases, the only difference is the annual rate of growth.

Case Study 3	Investing Amounts	Number of Years Investing	At 6% Growth	At 30% Growth
Married 50 Years old. High Income. Tax-Free Savings: £650,000	£14,400 per Year + Lump Sum of £650,000	10 Years	£1.4 Million	£9.9 Million

For the final time, let's extend the 10 year period to see what kinds of money could be made by the time this couple gets to age 65.

Because this couple are aged 50, we can do our projections on 15 years growth.

These next projections are based on each couple adding their full ISA allowance of £14,400 each and every year for a 15 year period and also growing their lump sum of £650,000 over that same 15 year period.

In this case, I have used a 15 year long-term growth target of 25%. Again, this is my best estimation of what is achievable over that length of time.

Investing £14,400 per Year at 25% + £650,000 Lump Sum at 25% (Growth over 15 Years)

When we hit calculate, the calculator quickly works out how much the saved £1200 per month would grow into if grown at 20% over the next 15 years and what the £650,000 lump sum would grow into if this was also grown at 20% over the next 15 years.

Here is the result:

Monthly Savings Plan

Find out how much a regular monthly savings scheme could make.

Monthly Payment £ 1200

Duration 15 **Years**

Interest Rate (annually) 25 %

RESULT Calculate >>

Your investment will be worth* £ 2,346,941.74

*This calculator assumes an initial balance of zero and that savings are made for a full month before interest is calculated and compounded.

Or Lump Sum Investments

Calculate how much a lump sum investment could be worth.

Amount Invested £ 650,000

Duration 15 **Years**

Interest Rate (annually) 25 %

RESULT Calculate >>

Your investment will be worth* £ 18,474,111.13

*This calculator assumes an initial balance of zero and that savings are made for a full year before interest is calculated and compounded.

Grand Total (Monthly and Lump Sum)

Your total investments will be worth £ 20,821,052.87

As you can see, the net result is a whopping twenty million, eight hundred and twenty one thousand, fifty two pounds and eighty seven pence.

And for the third time, let's summarise what we have just learned.

Case Study 3 - Summary

Case Study 3
Married 50 Years old.
High Income.
Tax-Free Savings: £650,000

Capital Invested	Projected Growth Rate	Length of Time Money Is Invested	Total Amount Money Grows Into
£14,400 per Year + Lump Sum of £650,000	6%	10 Years	£1.4 Million
£14,400 per Year + Lump Sum of £650,000	30%	10 Years	£9.9 Million
£14,400 per Year + Lump Sum of £650,000	25%	15 Years	£20.8 Million

As a final summary of the three case studies, you can see in this next table, each couple accumulates way above the £10 million pounds mark in tax-free income by age 65, which is a fair amount of money to have, by what is generally known as a benchmark for retirement.

Projection of Income by Age 65		
Case Study 1	**Case Study 2**	**Case Study 3**
Married 35 Years old. High Income. Tax-Free Savings: No.	Married 45 Years old. High Income. Tax-Free Savings: £250,000	Married 50 Years old. High Income. Tax-Free Savings: £650,000
£15.2 Million	**£13.4 Million**	**£20.8 Million**

And I am pretty sure that that kind of money would help you to create your dream lifestyle–or pretty close to it.

To help you clarify what you have just seen, if you and your partner make it a goal to do whatever you can to save the full ISA allowance each and every year, and you manage to get it to grow at significant rates of return, if you are starting from a similar financial position and / or you have time on your side, you and your partner could end up millions of pounds richer than you are today.

And that means you would be set up for life.

But you are probably saying something along the lines of, "Yes, Stephen, these figures are very appealing and *if* you could get your money to grow at high rates of return, of course it will grow into large amounts."

But HOW do you get these large growth rates? Is it really possible? In reality, could this really happen?

Yes, yes, yes … and I am going to prove it to you right now.

It is time to show you how my clients and I aim to get those greater than average tax-free returns so that you can do the same. If this sounds appealing you are going to love the next chapter. Get ready to discover…

CHAPTER 5

How to MAKE MILLIONS from the Up and Coming Stock Market Boom

"There is no line of endeavour in the world where real knowledge will pay as rich or as quick a monetary reward as Wall Street."
– Gerald Loeb

The information you are about to receive may change your life. You are about to learn a brand new way to invest. It's called ISA Trend Investing. As mentioned previously, this is a brand new approach to investing using ISAs. In the Introduction, you learned that there are 7 things that make this way of investing in ISAs different.

To remind you, when compared to normal ISA Investing, the 7 key differences are:

1. Instead of simply buying and holding, you are *active*. By understanding the overall trend or direction of the market, you invest into the market when the confirmation of the trend is up, and switch out of the market when the confirmation of the trend is down. This is the most important element in ISA Trend Investing.

This first difference is the one that will lead you to success if you get it right or failure if you get it wrong. Even if you find the best investment fund on the planet, if your trend reading is wrong, meaning your timing is wrong, you will fail.

2. You use a Stocks and Shares ISA instead of a Cash ISA.

3. When the trend is confirmed up, you look to buy the highest quality *Investment Funds*. You search for funds that can be purchased within a Stocks and Shares ISA. You do not buy individual stocks as they carry too much risk. You do not buy index tracker funds because it is possible to "beat" the indexes if you know what you are doing. You buy your fund or funds only when the market is healthy (uptrend). When the market is unhealthy (downtrend), you remain in a cash based fund.

4. When the market is healthy you time your buying of the fund or funds that you have selected. You only buy your fund or funds at the time where there is the maximum probability of success. To do this, you use technical analysis or charts.

5. You time your exits. When the market's trend is in a confirmed downtrend, **instead of selling and cashing in your ISA, you <u>switch</u>**. This helps you to move out of the downtrend so that you are completely

out of the market. This means your cash is now placed or "parked" in a Stocks and Shares cash based fund. You do this as soon as the market confirms its downtrend meaning the market is now unhealthy and unsafe to invest. This helps you to bank profits and *protect* and *preserve* your capital whilst the market is falling.

6. Because you can read the trend of the market, *and* pick the highest quality investment funds, it allows you to set yourself aggressive performance targets. You aim to beat the powerful US Nasdaq Composite. (The Nasdaq is capable of 24.5% annual returns over the long-term.)

7. You do not use an adviser. You become your own adviser and make your trades on a "smart" investing platform with virtually zero costs. By being your own adviser, you save on charges, commissions and initial set up fees. This seriously helps boost your overall compounded returns. And if you know what you are doing, you get much better results than you would if you were with an adviser.

With this method of investing in ISAs you also have the option of:

1) "Shadow" Investing successful ISA Trend Investors. This allows you to get exactly the same returns as they are getting and in a time friendly way.

2) SIPP Trend Investing. A SIPP (Self Invested Personal Pension) can be run parallel with your ISA Trend Investing. Whichever investment fund you buy with your ISA, you buy the same fund with your SIPP. That means if you get a 20% annual return on your ISA, you get a 20% annual return on your SIPP.

As well as sharing with you this unique way of investing using your ISA, I am going to give you more details about this investment opportunity which could help you retire rich. This same opportunity is right under everybody's noses but because they have not been informed about it, they have no idea it exists.

There is an English Proverb that sums this up beautifully: "*Some men go through a forest and see no firewood.*"

Okay, let's begin. To explain how it is possible to capitalise on this 10 year investment opportunity, we are going to start with some lessons on the stock market. Most Britons have heard of the FTSE 100 but fewer have heard of the S&P 500. The FTSE 100 is an index in the UK that has the top 100 companies trading in it.

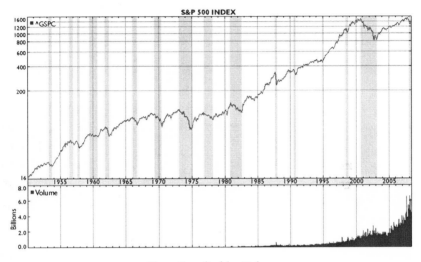

Data Supplied by Yahoo.

What long-term trend has this index formed? Is it up, down or sideways?

Yes, that's right, it's in an uptrend.

Can you see the grey vertical shaded areas on the chart?

These grey shaded areas are representing the down periods in the market. They are known as bear markets. And the white areas on this chart are the times when the market rose. These periods are called bull markets.

What do you see happening after each bear or down market?

That's right. The market goes up. Would you agree that after every bear market, the index always *eventually* moves into new high ground?

Good.

Did you know that historically, bull markets or up markets have lasted between two and four years?

Bear or down markets tend not to last as long. Bear markets tend to last between nine and eighteen months and therefore are much shorter than bull markets. Because bull markets last longer, the stock market forms an uptrend. It's like a staircase effect where you have three stairs up and then one stair down.

Just before we move on, take a look at the period on the chart from 1970 to 1980.

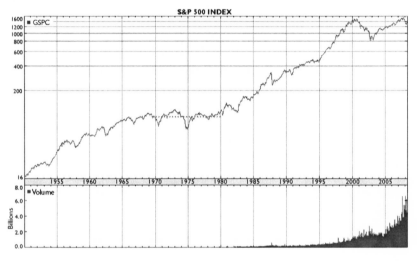

Data Supplied by Yahoo.

Notice that the market made very little price progress over that decade. Do you see that?

Do you also see what happened before it went sideways? Can you see the strong uptrend?

And what happened after 1980?

Do you see that after the 1970-1980 ten year period the market went on a nice run?

In other words, the market was in a strong uptrend, then it went sideways for ten years and then it resumed its uptrend.

Do you see that?

Good, because we will be talking more about that later.

Let's now move onto talking about funds. What do you know about investment funds?

In case you are unsure, an investment fund is a pooled investment vehicle that allows investors like you and me to invest in the stock market. They are controlled and managed by a professional investor who is called a fund manager. These fund managers buy stocks (companies) that they believe are going to rise in value. If they choose well, the fund's value will do well and all the people invested in the fund will be rewarded with an increase in their investment portfolio.

Investment Fund Managers Are Like Football Managers

Investment funds are the investment vehicles that have the power to grow your account at 20% per year if you choose well. Investment fund managers are like football managers. If you can find a fund manager with an outstanding track record you've cracked it. The challenge is that in the UK there are over one thousand ISA funds to choose from and so unless you know what you are doing and how to check various performance gauges, it is very easy to pick a dud fund.

To explain further we shall use British football manager, Sir Alex Ferguson as an example.

Let me ask you a question.

Sir Alex Ferguson is renowned for having a great track record.[65] What are the chances that he will do well next season?

The answer is, he will *probably* do well. Of course, there is no guarantee, but the probability of him performing well next season is pretty high.

That same principle applies to fund managers. In other words, when fund managers have great track records, they are also likely to keep doing well in the future, but as I've said, the challenge investors face is finding them.

Let's move on to ISAs.

ISAs are fantastic. Yes, they really are the UK's best-kept secret and it is not common knowledge about how they work or how powerful they are. Many people think that when they take out an ISA with a bank, their ISA has to remain with that same bank for life.

A few people mistakenly think that they are locked in and can't move it. Both these myths are utter nonsense.

With your ISAs, you have the power to control where your money is being parked or invested. And you can change your mind at any time. And if you have been placed in a Stocks and Shares ISA by your bank manager, broker or financial adviser, with a little training, it is really easy to check to see how good their recommendations have been.[66]

This is just one of the things my clients are taught when they become a member of the premium service we offer.

And when they have that knowledge, clients tell me that it makes their bank managers, brokers or advisers feel very nervous. Knowledge of the characteristics of a good fund versus the characteristics of a bad fund gives you serious power over your adviser.

Real ISA Millionaires

Most people in the UK are totally unaware that ISAs can help you accumulate a multi-million pound, tax-free portfolio.

However, some lucky people have already reaped the benefits. John Lee, a former Government minister, is one person who made over a million using his ISAs[67] and so are John and Judith Housden, a retired couple who live in Kent.[68]

And it was only recently that John Cotter, associate director of Barclays Stockbrokers said that some of his clients had built up ISA portfolios valued at over one million pounds.[69]

Did you know that an ISA is not an investment, but is the name of a wrapper that goes around an investment sheltering it from the Inland Revenue?

Think about a sweet in a wrapper. The investment is the sweet and the ISA is the wrapper.

Did you know that there is no limit to how much your tax-free pot can grow into?[70]

Yes, it's true. If you start with say, £1000 and eventually over time it grows into, let's say, £1 million, all of that £1 million would be tax-free.

Are you aware of the 2008 changes made to ISAs?

You should be because they may have affected you in a positive way. Now there are simply two types of ISAs; Cash ISAs and Stock and Shares ISAs.

Were you aware that it is possible to make 15% to 20% returns—instead of 5% or 6%—by simply transferring your Cash ISAs into Stocks and Shares ISAs?

Yes, it's true. <u>Any funds in existing Cash ISAs are transferable to a Stocks and Shares ISA</u>.

To put it another way, if you have built up a stock pile of Cash ISAs over the years, they can now be rolled into a Stocks and Shares ISA.

This is great news for anybody who has a desire to get 15-20% tax-free returns instead of 5% or 6% returns.

There were some other changes too. The Government stated that ISAs will continue to be made available beyond the original end date of April 2010.

And the annual limit that they allow you to invest per person was raised to £7200.

But the best announcement from the Government was this. They **publicly committed to ISAs for life**[71], rather than the previous 10 year period. This means you now have the security of knowing that the tax advantages will be long-term. ISAs are here to stay.

As mentioned on many occasions, one of the basics that I first learned about how the stock market works is that *three out of every four stocks move in the same direction as the market.*

So if the market is in an uptrend, three out of four stocks move up. And if the market is in a downtrend, three out of four stocks move down.

That tells you that when the market had an 80% correction between 2000 and 2002, individuals who remained invested in the market's downtrend over that period will have lost money.

As author and Wall Street stock wizard Vic Sperandeo states, *"The key to building wealth is to preserve capital and wait patiently for the right opportunity to make the extraordinary gains."*

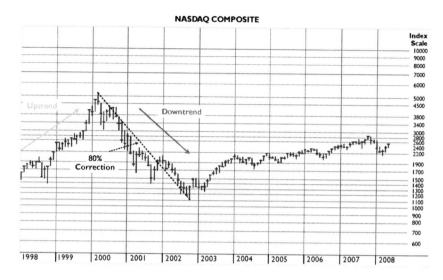

Data Supplied by Thomson Reuters.

Take a look at this chart of the Nasdaq.

On this chart I am showing you something important.

When the market was in a downtrend, the smart money was out on the sidelines.

Because investment funds own stocks, funds also move in the same trend or direction as the market.

You see, the market is like a river.

If it is flowing downwards, then you don't want to be in the river trying to swim upstream against a strong current.

And if the market is flowing downwards, you want to be on the sidelines patiently waiting for the flow of the river to change.

You therefore need to swim with the current and not against it.

Swim with the Stock Markets' Flow, Not Against It.
Image Courtesy of Getty Images.

To win at ISA Trend Investing, your job is to know how to pick a top performing investment fund and then wrap an ISA around it. You also need to make sure that you time your buying, meaning you buy it when the market is healthy—when the market is in an uptrend.

On the other hand, when the market goes into a downtrend, you need to switch out of your chosen investment fund and into a cash based fund.

William J. O'Neil is not well known in the UK, but in the US he is regarded as a stock market master.

As you learnt in Chapter 1, O'Neil taught me a proven timing system that helps you get in and get out of the market at the right time.[72] This timing system is based on helping you to determine future market direction.

It is also based on how the market in reality actually functions. Recently Bill commented on how far back they had gone when researching. He stated in a radio interview that they had tracked how the market operates in each of the market cycles over the last 125 years.[73]

But does it really work?

Not Missed the Start of EVERY Single Bull Market

As you heard in Chapter 1, using this system of timing the market, in the last 50 years Bill has not missed the start of *every* single bull market. That is pretty impressive isn't it? It is so impressive that I would like to say it again for emphasis:

Bill O'Neil, using this timing system has not missed the start of <u>every</u> single bull market over the last 50 years.

And it is no coincidence that this same timing system was the one that I used to time my first bull market in 2003.

In the spring of 2008, Bill said that the timing system he uses wasn't his. Instead he said that the system was based on how the market works.[74] What Bill also mentioned is that the way the market works is the same way it has worked throughout its entire history. And I agree. This is a very good point to highlight.

An Investment System Based on Facts, Not Opinions

<u>The timing system that Bill O'Neil uses and I use is based on facts</u> and therefore it's nobody's system. Yes, facts that have come from the entire 125 year history of the stock market and not opinions. That is probably why it tends to work so well. This same timing system also helped my clients and I to correctly get out at the end of the 2003-2007 bull market.[75] The market topped out in October 2007 and during the 3 month period that followed, the system my clients and I use to invest beat the Nasdaq by 21%.[76]

This was the period when the market fell 19% in just 3 months. However my clients and I were in a cash based fund which gained 2% over that same period.

As they say, timing is everything.

Personally I think it is a great way to accurately time the market.[77] But I have to warn you that it's not foolproof. When I read the trend of the market using this system, I get it right about 80-90% of the time.[78]

My clients follow in my footsteps. Clients like the fact that my brother Paul and I put our money where our mouth is. It puts them at ease when they find out my track record—and that they can follow exactly what Paul and I are doing with our ISA and SIPP investing. I think it gives them peace of mind knowing that Paul and I both have six figure plus, tax free accounts. They understand that the decisions Paul and I make personally about when to get into the market, what to get into and when to get out, are not taken lightly.

And unlike hedge funds, we don't take a penny of any of the profits our clients make. This means you get to keep everything you make. Plus we are totally impartial. Unlike financial advisers, stock brokers and banks, we do not receive any commission from the investment funds that we personally invest in. That's also something our clients see as a benefit.

Shadow Investing Helps You to Successfully Time the Market

We used to offer single year packages, which meant clients could shadow invest me over a 12 month period. These were selling after discounts at approximately £3000.[79] But now, new clients sign up for multi year support packages. These multi year shadow investing packages can be purchased in five, seven or ten year blocks.

The five year package is called *Financial Independence*. Its aim is to help you retire with a *comfortable* lifestyle. The seven year package is called the *Financial Freedom* package. This one helps you to retire with a *dream* lifestyle. This is when you reach a stage when money is no longer a worry.

Finally, the ten year package is called *Legacy Plus*. This is aimed at the seriously ambitious. In other words, people who want to create the ultimate in lifestyle choices. This is also for those who have a desire to pass on their wealth to others—such as helping your children get a great start in life.

All these packages offer shadow investing support.

This means you get to know directly from me if the market is healthy—and if the market is unhealthy.

You also learn what I am personally invested in so that you can do the same.

To put it another way, you can piggy back on my investment decisions and in turn get the same results as me. If I get 23%, so do you.

Let's continue.

Do you know the following fact?

75% of the stock market's movement comes from the big institutional investors.[80]

Yes it's true, the big professional investors have the largest influence on the market's future direction.

Institutional investors can be fund managers, banks, building societies or insurance companies. And if these 800 pound gorilla investors are buying, you can jump on to their coat-tails.

And if they are selling, you can quickly switch out on to the sidelines.

Here is how it works.

Picture the market as a big tree. Let's imagine the professional investors being woodcutters.

If the professionals are selling heavily, you can see them selling their stocks by looking at charts.

**The Big Professional Investors
Are Like WoodCutters.**
Image Courtesy of Getty Images.

When they sell, it is like them taking a cut out of a tree and this of course makes the tree or market weaker.

If they take too many swipes at the tree in a short space of time, what is going to happen?

That's right, the tree will fall over. So when the tree or market gets weak because of excessive selling or cutting, it sends you a red flag to say get out of the market. On the other hand, when the professional investors are buying heavily and in a short period of time, this makes the market healthy and extremely strong–and this is the time when you do want to be invested.

If you become a client, you receive *Daily Market Updates* and you will get five of these delivered directly to your email tray each and every week. That's one for every day the market is open. Each *Daily Market Update* has a symbol at the top to quickly let you know what is going on. As you can see, we use a green, smiley face if the market is healthy and we use a red, unhappy face if the market is unhealthy. In a typical year, I would make no more than four switches in and out of the market. This helps to make the system extremely time friendly.

The Nasdaq over the last 25 years has averaged 18.3%. And as previously mentioned, if during the last 10 years it had continued that trend, by the end of 2007, it would have been trading at 8433 instead of 2652.

... but over the last ten years, as you can see from this chart, it has virtually moved sideways.

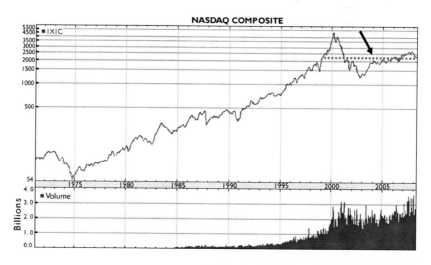

Data Supplied by Yahoo.

Let me repeat once again for emphasis. Over the last 10 years, the Nasdaq has been underperforming its long-term trend and therefore could be due a move. Plus this move might be substantial and powerful because at the moment, the market (on the chart below) looks like it has formed a very bullish cup-with-handle formation. And that means it could be ready to begin moving northwards at any time.

Could there be a possible stock market boom on the horizon?

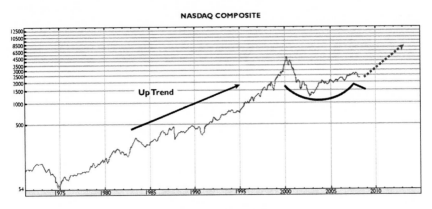

NASDAQ COMPOSITE

Data Supplied by Yahoo.

You see, as my brother Paul mentioned in his Note to the Reader, a "cup-with-handle" is an investment term for a price chart pattern that stocks and indexes form just *before* they take off on major runs. They start with a powerful uptrend and at some point they have to rest and therefore correct in price before eventually proceeding to even higher ground. The cup-with-handle is known to be the one pattern that produces the most powerful and sustained moves.

Is it any wonder my clients and I are so excited right now?

It is also good to remind you at this point how strong the Nasdaq can be over a ten year period. As you heard earlier, from 1990 to 2000 the Nasdaq went up on average 24.5% per year and the great news is that because it's done it before, it can do it again. In case you forgot, the Nasdaq Composite is the US technology index.

Did you know that the Nasdaq Composite is one of the world's leading market indexes?

It is, and because it's a world leader, it is one of the reasons why we try to beat it each and every year. In other words, it is very tough to beat. What we like about it is that it provides us with a challenge.

An Investment System Capable of Beating the Nasdaq

In other words, the Nasdaq is a great benchmark and it is much more difficult to beat than the S&P 500 which is the index that most professional fund managers try to beat. And here is the good bit. **What we now know is that the system my clients and I use is capable of beating the Nasdaq**[81] and I am going to show you evidence of this in a moment, so you don't have to take my word for it.

Let me give you a quick example. As previously mentioned, the very first fund that our screening tool (HIRE CAR™) found was called the AXA Framlington Japan Fund. HIRE CAR™ found it in 2003.

● Fund: AXA Framlington Japan Fund Acc

	2000	2001	2002	2003	2004	2005	2006	31/07
Total Return	-29.29	-40.30	-22.95	91.05	28.74	46.91	-12.63	-2.90

Data Supplied by Morningstar.

To remind you, the AXA Framlington Japan Fund was the Number 1 performing fund in 2003, returning 91.05%. The Nasdaq that same year returned 50%.

Was it a fluke that we found and invested in the Number 1 performing fund of 2003? Was it luck?

HIRE CAR™; a Secret Formula for Finding Winning Funds

My clients don't think so. You see, the following year, in 2004, the system helped our accounts beat the Nasdaq fourfold and in 2005 we beat the Nasdaq by tenfold. You might be wondering how could we beat the Nasdaq by so much and the answer is simple. HIRE CAR™ has an almost uncanny way of picking up on its radar exactly where the big money is flowing.

So what funds did HIRE CAR™ uncover after 2003?

As you may recall, HIRE CAR™ helped us find AND also invest in the Number 1 and the Number 3 top performing funds over the 2003-2007 bull market.

The Number 1 performing fund of the 2003-2007 bull market is called the Invesco Perpetual Latin America Fund. It gained 587.8%, beating the Nasdaq by almost six times and averaging 47% per year over that 5 year period.

The Number 3 performing fund of the 2003-2007 bull market is called the Scottish Widows Latin America Fund. This one gained 492.3%, beating the Nasdaq by almost five times and averaging 42.7% per year over that 5 year period.

We will be looking closer at these two funds later.

This timing system also works quite well on the downside. For example, in 2004 the Nasdaq had a massive 19% correction (almost a new bear market) but HIRE CAR™ helped us make a one year gain of 32.5%.[82]

Plus the system correctly predicted the end of the 2003-2007 bull market. It helped us to quickly move out of the market. This was when the market fell a nasty 24.7%. Anybody in the market over that time will have nursed some serious losses.

And if we go back to how the system performs on the upside, when we look at what happened in the last quarter of 2006 and the first quarter of 2007, I called many of my clients to make sure that they had bagged the same gain that I'd got.

I was thrilled when almost all of them stated that over the four month period their ISA accounts had seen increases of over 18% versus the Nasdaq's 6% move. This means that over that 16 week time slot, <u>we tripled the Nasdaq's performance</u>.

Return Annually 20% on Your Capital

In a moment, I am going to show you the fund that my clients and I invested in to get that 18% gain.

But first I want you to understand that this was the same fund featured in the *Daily Market Updates* that my clients were receiving each day.

And because the Nasdaq has the capability to grow at an average yearly return of 18.3% it indicates that if you use a system that can beat the Nasdaq, logic tells you that over the long-term, you are probably going to annualise 20% or more on your capital.

Some people want to know how we are doing against the Nasdaq this year. In other words, is HIRE CAR™ beating it right now?

The short answer to that is yes, it is. At the time of writing this book, the ISA Trend Investing System we use is beating the Nasdaq by a very respectable 12.1%.[83]

Before we move on, let me tell you a little more about HIRE CAR™.

**HIRE CAR™, a Secret
Investing Formula.**
Image Courtesy of Getty Images.

HIRE CAR™ is my secret investing formula. <u>Since it was created, it has proved that it can beat the powerful Nasdaq Composite</u>.[84]

People say that HIRE CAR™ is perhaps the most effective investment fund screening tool ever developed. It is a seven step process for finding the best of the best investment funds. And the way it continually discovers these funds continues to amaze even the most sceptical people. The name HIRE CAR™ is an acronym. Each of the seven letters in HIRE CAR™ represents an important part of the formula. We will talk more about HIRE CAR™ in a moment.

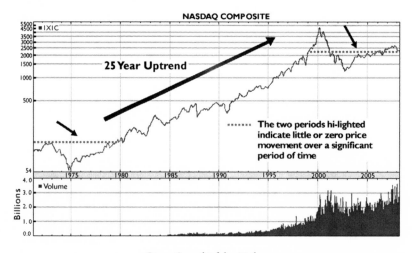

Data Supplied by Yahoo.

Here is a chart similar to one that I showed you earlier. This chart clearly shows the investment opportunity that we've been talking about. Can you see on this chart that the Nasdaq has had a nice 25 year run up from 1975 to 2000?

Over that period, it actually grew by an impressive 8750%.[85] As we established earlier, the Nasdaq has underperformed over the last 10 years and when markets move sideways for long periods, sooner or later, they have to resume their upward advances.

Look at the period on the chart recording the Nasdaq's price performance from 1970 to 1980.

After that sideways movement, what did it do?

That's right; it went on a nice run.

When Will the Market Move?

You see, with the Nasdaq being capable of 24.5% annual returns over a decade, my clients and I are feeling optimistic about it putting in a similar performance … or even better over the next 10 years.

When will the move start, you may be asking. Well it could have just begun. For now, all you need to know is that the market will make its move when it is good and ready and when it does make its move, you want to be there to catch it.

Because I watch the market like a hawk, and I watch it each and every day, when it does start its move, my clients and I can and will get in right near the start. And I suggest, my friend, that you consider being part of that move too.

Are you starting to see how this next ten year period could be an opportunity to make some decent tax-free money?

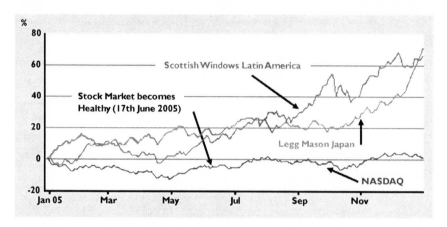

Data Supplied by Financial Express.

This chart shows two investment funds that HIRE CAR™ found from the thousand plus funds out there. These are funds that my clients and I actually invested in and made money from.

Let me explain how HIRE CAR™ works.

HIRE CAR™ works like a radar–scanning for the funds that are managed by the best fund managers.

HIRE CAR™ also picks up on where the big money is flowing. Through a rigorous screening process, HIRE CAR™ looks at all the ISA investment funds and then screens each one to make sure it passes the strict set criteria. By the way, only about 0.5% actually make the grade because HIRE CAR™ is so tough to pass.[86]

It Was So Beautiful

We will be talking more about the Scottish Widows Latin America Fund later but for now let me take this opportunity to mention the Legg Mason Japan Fund. When I think about the time this fund took off like a rocket, I always smile. It was so beautiful. You see, just after we bought it, it surged 49.7% in 12 weeks.

Notice how powerful these two funds are when compared against the extremely strong Nasdaq. Do you see how both of them easily outperform it?

Are you starting to see how this system works?

Next, I want to show you two funds that have been mentioned previously. These are funds that HIRE CAR™ uncovered and they turned out to be the Number 1 and Number 3 top performers of the 2003-2007 bull market.

● Fund: Scottish Widows Latin America Fund A Acc

	2001	2002	2003	2004	2005	2006	2007	31/03
Total Return	0.63	-28.28	50.63	28.92	66.97	27.24	43.57	-4.02

Data Supplied by Morningstar.

The Scottish Widows Latin America Fund was the Number 3 top performing fund of the 2003-2007 bull market. This fund averaged 42.7% per year over that 5 year period.

It was also the fund that my clients and I got into over that four month period I mentioned earlier—when we made over 18%.

Notice the gains it's made each year over the last five.

Let's now move on to another great example.

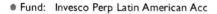

			2001	2002	2003	2004	2005	2006	2007	31/03
Total Return			-8 68	-34 27	81.02	31.32	67.93	25.95	36.82	-5.40

Data Supplied by Morningstar.

This second one has also been kind to my clients and me. It was the Number 1 performing fund of the 2003-2007 bull market. It is called the Invesco Perpetual Latin American Fund.

This one beat the Nasdaq by almost six times and averaged 47% per year over that 5 year period.

This is the fund Paul and I used for our SIPP accounts—and it helped them to grow by 60% in just two years.[87]

Once again, notice the gains that it's made each year over the last five.

A Quick Word of Caution

Did you know that these sorts of funds were available for people like you and me to invest in?

Well they are—and these are the types of funds that HIRE CAR™ helps you to find, but before you go rushing out to buy such a fund, here is a quick word of caution.

These kinds of funds must only be purchased in the right market environments.

They can also drop very quickly so getting your timing right is crucial.

Knowing if the market is healthy and in an <u>uptrend</u> is vital when purchasing one of these types of funds.

Now you've been shown a possible investment opportunity of a lifetime, let me ask you some questions.

- Can you see now how it is possible to return greater than average tax-free returns using ISA Trend Investing?

  In other words, getting into the best performing funds on strength and out onto the sidelines in weakness?

- Can you also see how it is possible (depending upon your starting point) to make millions of pounds in tax-free money over the next 10 years, especially if the market does have a strong and powerful move to the upside?

- And can you agree that the market may indeed have this strong 10 year period because the last 10 years on the market have been pretty much flat?

I hope you said yes to all three because if you did, it means that you and I, my friend, are singing from the same hymn sheet.

Retiring Rich Has Its Benefits.
Image Courtesy of Getty Images.

And let me now ask you another question:

Do you like this new way to invest using your ISA allowance?

If you said no, I am sorry that it doesn't appeal to you and now is the time to bid each other farewell. However, if you are like most people, you probably liked what you have seen and want to know more.

If this is the case, you now have two options.

We'll explore what these two routes are in the next chapter.

Are you still buzzing?

I hope so because you are about to learn how it's possible to…

CHAPTER 6

Retire Rich in Just 3 Minutes per Day

"The greatest source of leverage is other people."
– Richard Koch

If you like what I've just shown you, you now have two options. The first is to do it yourself and the second is to get some help.

Which Route Is Best for You?
Image Courtesy of Getty Images.

Route 1 - DIY Approach

You now know that to profit from the stock market over the next ten, twenty or even thirty years, it's all about being able to:

a) Find the best of the best investment vehicles consistently.

b) Accurately and consistently interpret the *trend* of the market so that you can get into the market on strength and get out on weakness.

c) Beat the Nasdaq over the long-term.

d) Get greater than average tax-free returns over the long-term.

Therefore, you now need to answer the following questions.

Do you know how to:

a) Find the best of the best investment vehicles consistently?

b) Accurately and consistently interpret the *trend* of the market so that you can get into the market on strength and get out on weakness?

c) Beat the Nasdaq over the long-term?

d) Get greater than average tax-free returns over the long-term?

If you are confident that the answers are yes, the do it yourself approach is probably for you and you will not need any help.

Here is a quick word of advice.

If you do go down the DIY route, please ensure that you fully understand who you will be going up against.

Warren Buffett, regarded as one of the world's greatest stock market investors, sends this word of caution:

"The market, like the Lord, helps those who help themselves. But, unlike the Lord, the market does not forgive those who know not what they do."

I therefore suggest that it might not be the best of ideas to cut corners.

In other words, if you are going to take this do it yourself approach seriously, please commit to putting in the hours needed to succeed.

I like to use the game of rugby to explain what I mean.

You Could Get Hurt.
Image Courtesy of Getty Images.

When investing in the market, you are going up against professionals. Imagine a person who has not played rugby before going head to head with professional rugby players. What would happen?

If you thought pain, you would be right on the money.

And so please bear this in mind. Being unprepared and uneducated could cost you dearly. I suggest you make a decision to put in the hours if you are going to go down the DIY route, get help or scrap the whole thing.

A moment ago, I asked you four questions. If you answered "no" to all of them, you now have two more choices.

1. Learn how to do it on your own.

2. Get help.

If you want to learn how to do this yourself, it will take effort, discipline and a lot of time.

But ... it is possible.

If you are thinking of taking the solo route, the first thing that you would need to discover is how to become very good at reading the trend of the market as well as how to find the top performing funds. To give you an idea, it takes a person around 10,000 hours to master the trend of the market.[88] That is the equivalent of learning and studying the market for 40 hours a week for the next 5 years. To become an expert in fund selection, it is going to take you at least 12 months to become highly proficient.

Do You Really Want to Become a Full-Time Stock Market Professional?

And so you need to ask yourself:

Do you have the time and intense desire to do whatever it takes (time, effort, sacrifice, financial resources etc.) to become a stock market and investment fund professional?

If the answer is yes, once again you will not need any help. And if you did answer yes, in Chapter 9 I will give you a complete outline of the steps you can take to get you on the fast road to becoming a full-time stock market professional.

Route 2 - Get Help

On the other hand, about 95% of the people I speak to do not want to do it themselves. Because they have busy lives and no real desire to become a stock market professional, they often think it is a better idea to get help from a person or company who knows what they are doing.

Help can come in the form of accountants, IFA's, stock brokers, banks, financial educators or professional stock market investors.

And if you remember what I said in the introduction:

"However, at the end of the day, we have to remember that it's all about results. You want to be teamed up with a person who can deliver the goods year in, year out. In other words, if your financial adviser, broker or bank's advice has helped you to beat the market over the long-term, you've found yourself an outstanding contact.

But if he or she has not helped you to beat the market over the long-term, it may be time to look for an alternative."

With this in mind, combined with what you have just learned, you can now ask the questions:

Does my current adviser know how to:

a) Find the best of the best investment vehicles consistently?

b) Accurately and consistently interpret the *trend* of the market so that you can get into the market on strength and get out on weakness?

c) Beat the Nasdaq over the long-term?

d) Get greater than average tax-free returns over the long-term?

If the answer is yes, the best decision would be to stick with who you have. But if they aren't delivering the goods, then it could be time to look at making a change.

Some people opt to tap into the expertise of successful stock market investors. And the main reason for this is because it can increase their probability of success, as well as saving them time *and* money.

And if you are like me, you'll believe that time is far more valuable than money.

As motivational speaker, philosopher and entrepreneur Jim Rohn once wrote, *"Today does not care about yesterday's failures or tomorrow's regrets. It merely offers the same precious gift —another 24 hours—and hopes that we will use it wisely."*

Okay so you've had a bit of time to think about which route will suit you best, which way are you thinking of taking?

Are you thinking of doing this yourself or do you want to know how I might be able to help you?

An ISA Shadow Investing Solution That You Might Like

If you are thinking of getting help, let me tell you about one option to consider. Shadow investing is what a lot of my clients call the lazy man's route to riches—and it may be just what you've been looking for. And the good news is that if you take this route, it is a solution that takes just 3 minutes per day.

It is called the Tax-Free Millionaire Shadow Investing System.

The Tax-Free Millionaire Shadow Investing System can play an essential part in helping you to retire rich.

What Is It? And How Does It Work?

Let me quickly explain what the Tax-Free Millionaire System is and how it works to see if you like it.

First of all, take a look at this model.

It illustrates what ISA Trend Investing is and shows you the two options available. To win, you can either take a DIY approach or a Get Help approach.

ISACO's ISA Trend Investing System

Route 1 - Do It Yourself	Route 2 - "Shadow" Invest
Step 1 - Determine Market Health	Steps 1, 2 and 3 are executed by Stephen Sutherland.
If the market is healthy 😊 move to step 2.	You have the option of simply following his lead.
If the market is unhealthy 🙁 remain in cash.	On your behalf, Stephen and his professional resources:
Step 2 - Find a Fund	**A)** Reads the market health
If the market is healthy, search and find a high quality ISA investment fund.	**B)** If healthy, he finds a high quality ISA investment fund or funds using HIRE CAR™
Step 3 - Time Your Buy / Exits	**C)** He buys the investment fund or funds at the optimum time
You buy your ISA investment fund at the optimum time where there is the highest probability of success.	**D)** He accurately exits the fund at the optimum time to lock in profits
You accurately time your exits – You "switch" out of your fund when the fund or market is unhealthy.	Note: ISACO's Shadow Investing System takes just 3 minutes per day

From studying the model, you may have noticed that with Route 2, it is unique.

Accountants, financial advisers, stock brokers and banks do not offer this shadow investing 3 step system.

And as I just mentioned, **this simple 3 step process takes you no more than 3 minutes per day to work.** In summary, the Tax-Free Millionaire System helps you to get greater than average tax-free returns. What you get is a combination of time friendly education plus a way of shadow investing what I am doing with my ISA and SIPP account. By signing up to this package you would automatically become an ISACO premium client. By the way, ISACO is the company that my brother and I founded back in 2001.

Learn the Secrets of HIRE CAR; A Fast Easy Way to Locate the Very Best Investment Funds

If you decided that this package was for you, your education would start by learning about my secret formula; HIRE CAR™.

As you have discovered, HIRE CAR™ is a fund screening tool that helps you to quickly find outstanding rare funds, capable of powerful future returns.

And how it works is really simple. Let me explain. When the market is healthy, <u>HIRE CAR™ helps you to quickly locate and profit from where the big money is being invested</u>.

To explain what I mean, when the market is healthy, you ALWAYS want to be invested in funds that are classed as the best. This means you have a high probability of outperforming the Nasdaq, helping you to score superior investment returns over the long-term.

You see, when you use HIRE CAR™ to find the best investment opportunities, you are invested in funds that own the market's leading stocks.

These leading stocks are companies that blaze the trail northwards; ones that make the biggest price moves. And because your chosen fund or funds own these leading stocks, as these leaders surge forward, the fund or funds you own will also surge forward–and so will your ISA and SIPP accounts.

To clarify, *if* HIRE CAR™ discovers that the big money is flowing into the USA, HIRE CAR™ will pick that up on its radar and then proceed to find the best of the best of the funds invested in the USA.

Or if the flow of money is going into one of the developing nations such as China, India or South America, HIRE CAR™ will spot that too and once again home in on the very best funds, ones with the highest probability of performing well once you've bought them.

And the great thing about this is that you will be participating indirectly in the growth of the countries or continents where the serious money is flowing into–but have complete peace of mind knowing that your cash is held by a UK regulated company and can be accessed whenever you wish.

Plus…there is more.

Also with this package, you discover the golden rules of HIRE CAR™ that when followed, maximize your probability of success.

ISA Shadow Investing–in Just 3 Minutes per Day

As well as being educated in how the system works, you would also get a support package that tells you on a daily basis what I am doing with my tax-free money (my ISAs and SIPP). This means you can follow directly in my footsteps. The Tax-Free Millionaire System provides you with a fly on the wall view of what I am doing with my tax-free investments so that you can do the same.

It's like being able to look over my shoulder–to see exactly what I am doing so that you can follow my lead day by day, week by week, month by month and year by year.

This means you will be able to get almost identical returns to what I am getting and all in just three minutes per day. Through this system, you get to learn the secret HIRE CAR™ formula, how it works and the 9 Golden Rules that govern it. By sticking with this system over the long-term it's not a question of *if* you will get to your goals but more a question of *when*. If you simply follow the rules of the system, you will be literally guaranteeing that you retire liquid rich.

The way you shadow invest me is simply by reading electronic daily reports called *Daily Market Updates* (DMUs) and a monthly newsletter called *The Big Picture*.

Reading a *Daily Market Update* is a little bit like receiving a personal telephone call from me to tell you what I'm thinking about the market and more importantly, what I'm actually *doing* so that you can do the same.

Why it Takes You Just 3 Minutes per Day to Retire Rich

The 3 minutes per day promise is based on the amount of time it takes you to read your *Daily Market Update*. <u>The length of time it takes to read a *Daily Market Update* has been timed—and it really does take less than 3 minutes.</u>

Now you might be asking what happens after reading it. To answer, <u>in 98-99% of cases, your *Daily Market Update* will arrive in your inbox, you'll read it and you'll have no action to take.</u>

You see, most of the time you and I will be invested in the stock market, sitting tight in winning funds, watching the market rise and our tax-free accounts slowly increase in value. But there will be other times when the market will be falling—and to protect and preserve our capital, we'll simply sit on the sidelines in cash.

In both these cases, whether the market is rising or falling, you'll simply read your update and take no action.

But on a few rare occasions during the year, you will have some action to take. This is when you'd make a *switch* either into the market or out of the market–depending on what the market was doing. Remember, you'd be shadow investing me, so you'd simply follow my lead.

Finally, you might be pleased to hear that ISACO offers a no questions asked, 30 day, money back guarantee, just in case you came on board and discovered you didn't find this service of value or that it wasn't just three minutes per day. Incidentally, in all the years since our company began, back in 2001, **not one person has ever said to me that the system takes more than 3 minutes per day**–and when you read what my clients say about this way of investing (for example in Appendix A - found at the back of this book), you'll find they continually comment on its time friendly nature.

You Get to Know What I am Personally Invested in So That You Can Do the Same

The *Daily Market Update* (DMU) is the only stock market report in the world that informs you of whether I believe it's *safe* to invest and where the smart and intelligent money is being invested right now. From this service, <u>I do all the work on your behalf</u> which means that you get to spend your time doing what you love to do. This might include building your business, reading or even writing a book, travel, spending time with your family, working out at the gym or enjoying a round of golf with friends.

Plus, when you are a client of mine, my brother Paul immediately assigns you your very own consultant, whose job it is to help you set up your account through a *smart* trading platform. A smart trading platform is simply a way to control your account online from the comfort of your own home. It is smart because it's a way to almost completely remove unnecessary fees and expenses.

Your personal consultant will show you how to drastically reduce or completely remove financial adviser costs, set-up fees, annual fees and switching charges. His or her job is to make sure that they do everything in their power to get you up and running fast and with zero charges.

Many people ask me:

"Who is this package specifically aimed at?"

And as I said earlier in the book, this is how I answer:

Hungry, ambitious individuals who want to retire rich and have one or more of the following motivations for retiring wealthy:

- Financial Security in Retirement.

- A Better Personal Lifestyle.

- Desire to Enjoy the Finer Things in Life.

- Being Able to Travel Extensively.

- Financial Security for the Children.

- Early Retirement.

- Being Able to Afford a Large Property in an Affluent Area.

- Private Education for the Children.

- The Enjoyment of Making Money.

- Being Able to Help Others.

- Status.

- Owning More Than One Property.

Even though people know I take good care of all my clients,[89] some people want to know who these clients are. Many of my clients are like me. **They started with nothing and now have a six figure account.** Some of them have seven figure accounts.

And it is only a matter of time before their six figure, tax-free accounts become seven and seven figure accounts become eight—especially with the market being due a move.

As mentioned in the "About the Author" section, my list of clients includes aspiring millionaires, millionaires and multi-millionaires. They come from varied backgrounds. They include executives, CEOs, managing directors, business owners, entrepreneurs, pioneers, property investors, sports celebrities and professionals such as doctors, dentists and lawyers.

For example, I have the Chair of Trustees who manages a £550 million pound pension fund on my books, the Chief Information Officer of a FTSE 250 financial company, the original pioneer of health clubs in the UK, a dentist who is a leading authority in cosmetic, implant and restorative dentistry, a professional rugby player, a hedge fund manager and two serial property investors who at the last count owned 150 properties between them.

With the Tax-Free Millionaire System, You Learn:

- The Foundations for Building Lasting Wealth

- The Secret Formula–The Complete Step by Step System of How to Retire "Liquid" Rich in Just 3 Minutes per Day

- How the 3 Minutes per Day Shadow Investing System Makes the Whole Process Easy and Thoroughly Enjoyable

- A Unique Screening Tool That Can Help You Find Investment Funds with the Capability of Returning 47% per Annum over a 5 Year Period

- How Professional Investors Use Tax-Shelters to Their Advantage

- How to Quickly Locate Investment Funds That Could Help You Double Your Money in Just a Couple of Years

- How Top-Drawer Investors Manage Their Investments Funds

- When to Buy at the Right Time

- When to Sell So That You Can Protect Your Profits

- The Secret of the Wealthy

7 Reasons to Choose the Tax-Free Millionaire Shadow Investing System:

1. A Unique Way of Following in the Footsteps of a Pro Investor - Normally, whenever you sign up for any kind of wealth building educational package, you pay, you learn and then you apply. With this package, you get more. Just one of the differences lies in the Shadow Investing service that you receive after your learning is complete.

You get a subscription to the *Daily Market Update* and *The Big Picture*, which collectively help you to follow in my footsteps and all **in just 3 minutes per day.** You also get assigned your very own consultant who will be right by your side to get you quickly up and running.

2. Personalised Information That Is Easy to Understand and Apply - After you have completed your learning on how the system works, you will get an opportunity to ask any questions you might have. Plus the package has been created and written by me in basic English. This makes all the information that I share with you easy to understand.

3. Money-Back Guarantee - There is no risk. If you decide to come on board and become a client, and for any reason during the first 30 days of membership, the package does not meet your expectations, or you don't find the Tax-Free Millionaire package value for money, or you don't find that the system really is 3 minutes per day, **you can ask for a FULL REFUND, no questions asked.**

Therefore the risk lies with us instead of with you.

The good news is that there is a very high probability that you will be completely delighted by the overall package. 91% of people who sign up say they would heartily recommend it to others.[90]

4. Great Value - You will find that this cutting-edge information plus high level support package is not only affordable but great value too.

5. It Is Filled with Valuable Information - You are not going to find another package anywhere in the world where you will learn and have access to an easy to understand, 3 minutes per day, wealth-producing & protecting, tax-free investment system. And the information is presented in a way to maximize retention so that you remember much more of what you have learned.

6. Outstanding Networking Opportunity–For Both Business and Pleasure – When you become a client, you get the benefit of teaming up with my other clients.

These are ambitious people who want the same things out of life as you do. It is a wonderful opportunity to build new friendships with like-minded companions (friendships that often last for years…maybe for the rest of your life).

7. This Package Provides a Gateway to *The Liquid Club* - By signing up, you automatically receive membership to the exclusive *Liquid Club*. The club's mission is to help each and every club member to *Retire Liquid Rich*.

To summarise, the package is therefore a combination of 3 things.

Number 1 - You Discover the SECRETS of the System

The first thing you learn is how the Tax-Free Millionaire System works.

You receive a ***Tax-Free Millionaire Manual***–written by me–which includes everything you need to know about the 3 minutes per day shadow investing system. The information presented in your manual includes the unique screening tool HIRE CAR™–which will help you to find the best of the best investment funds; where the big money is flowing into.

Number 2 - The Ability to Shadow Invest a Pro Investor

The second thing you get is a subscription to the *Daily Market Updates* and a monthly newsletter called *The Big Picture*. This is the electronic support that tells you what I'm doing with my tax-free money so that you can do the same.

You get 241 *Daily Market Updates* and 12 editions of *The Big Picture* which keep you informed on a daily basis when I believe it is safe to invest, when I am buying, what I am buying and when I am switching into safe investment vehicles.

Normally, the maximum amount of trades or switches that I make over a 12 month period is four. This tells you that your level of activity is going to be extremely low, making it very time friendly. It is a nice way of getting greater than average tax-free returns–by simply looking at a daily email that takes no more than 3 minutes per day to read.

Number 3 - Membership to *The Liquid Club*

The third thing you get is membership to the exclusive *Liquid Club*. This is a private, members-only club where each member shares the common goal: to retire *Liquid* rich.

Learn the Secrets of How the System Works— In Under 2 Hours—from the Comfort of Your Own Home

Some people ask how the training is delivered. The answer is that <u>you learn how the system works from the comfort of your own home or office. This means you do not have to attend a multi day seminar as you do when learning other investment systems.</u>

This saves you money on travel and overnight accommodation plus you don't have to spend precious time away from your family. With no travel involved, you also do your bit for the environment by keeping your carbon footprint in check.

In keeping with our time friendly philosophy, you get fully up to speed with how the system works in less than 2 hours.[91]

Once you have discovered the secrets of the system, you will then be switched on to the *Daily Market Updates*.

These electronic updates allow you to shadow invest exactly what I am doing with my money. If I make 23% for the year, so do you.

By the way, <u>you will need fast access to £20,000 or more in liquid to take advantage of this premium shadow investing service.</u>

When You Google Us, You Will Discover Positive Comments, Transparency and Total Integrity

Just so that you are aware, if an individual is thinking of signing up for the premium package—and they contact my brother Paul for more details, he explains that the first step is for him to find out more about them. This usually takes no more than 3-5 minutes and he does this over the phone.

During this brief chat, Paul discovers their financial situation. And as I just mentioned, **you need at least £20,000 in liquid to take full**

advantage of the shadow investing service. Whilst Paul has to screen financially, he also checks for compatibility. In other words, do we have a values match?

By the way, if you are thinking of the possibility of signing up for the shadow investing system, <u>you should always do background checks and Google me, Paul and our company, in order to feel more comfortable about doing some business with us</u>.

Background checks is something I actively encourage you to do. You see, as soon as your research on us starts to reveal integrity and total congruency, you are going to feel confident about teaming up with us.

The process of checking to see if people have the financial means–and that there is a high probability that we will all get on well–is a win for you and us. We win because we get to help genuinely nice people to retire rich; helping their dream lifestyle to become a reality. That gives us a great sense of pleasure.

When You Become a Client, You Get VIP Treatment

And it is a big win for you, because you get a superb service where you are treated like a VIP right from the start. Plus I can make introductions to some high profile people on your behalf that could turn out to be very helpful in reaching your financial or business goals.

This means you get to meet and become friends with other like-minded individuals–who have also been carefully selected. And because you and I will be sharing a long-term view rather than that of a single transaction, it will help to get our business relationship off to a great start.

This is great for you because the longer you stay with us, the more we get to know you and your family on a more personal level, and you never know, we may become close friends. This, I feel, is a great way to conduct business. I like warmth between people. I like to connect. I like to bond.

Our credo is **people first, products second and profits third.** Most financial institutions, including many financial training companies, are unfortunately flawed by thinking transaction rather than long-term relationship.

Please Be Aware! - We Have to Limit the Number of Clients Who Shadow Invest Me

Oh, and just one final key note. If you are seriously thinking about becoming a client, you need to know this.

We only have a limited number of spaces available for the shadow investing service that our company offers. This means entrance to the club is on a first come first served basis.

Why?

We can only serve a limited number of clients due to possible future liquidity challenges. At the moment, we do not have any such challenges— because the amount of money that is following in my footsteps is of a safe level. This allows the service to work effectively. To put it another way, all clients can safely get into the same funds as I do, on the same day and they can also safely get out of the funds, the same day I do.

Even though I make it very clear that I do not give financial advice, I always like to operate in a responsible manner. My goal therefore is to ensure that all clients' orders are filled on both the buy and the sell side.

If there are too many people following my lead, meaning that there is too much money wanting to get into the same investment funds as me, it could cause a challenge.

If the investment fund or funds can't handle that level of business, it means that I or a client may:

a) Not get filled with a buy order which means a person or persons could miss a move.

b) Not get filled with a sell order which would mean a person or persons could be trapped in an investment when really they should be out on the sidelines. This is called a *squeeze* and it is a very unpleasant experience.

Because my clients have started to spread the word about this unique service that we offer, the business' growth has started to accelerate. This means that it might not be that long before all the shadow investing places are taken.

In the next chapter, I am going to show you how it is possible to read the market like the pros. I'm going to let you into all the tips, strategies and techniques that they use and I use to build substantial amounts of wealth.

And by mastering the skill of being able to read the market, it can help you in two ways. First, if you are going down the DIY route, it will give you massive insights into how and what you will need to do to master future market direction. On the other hand, if you are possibly thinking of wanting to shadow invest me, you will see how my own personal analysis of the market is based on science instead of guess work.

This one is going to really get you going. Enjoy.

CHAPTER 7

How to Read the Market Like the Professionals

"*The stock market is the greatest, most complex puzzle ever invented and it pays the biggest jackpot.*"
– Jesse Livermore

You can choose the best investment fund in the world but if you invest in it and you are wrong about the trend of the market, your portfolio is going to suffer. This happened to thousands of uninformed people in the great bear market of 2000-2002 and in the bear market that started in the last quarter of 2007.

With ISA Trend Investing, **getting your timing right is crucial.** Many people mistakenly think that it is all about choosing the best investment fund to park your money in. Whilst finding a high quality fund is important, it's not as important as getting in sync with the market's trend. As a reminder, here is what I mentioned earlier about how timing the market fits in with this new approach to ISA investing.

Instead of simply buying and holding, you are active. By understanding the overall trend or direction of the market, you invest into the market when the confirmation of the trend is up, and switch out of the market when the confirmation of the trend is down. This is the most important element in ISA Trend Investing.

This first difference is the one that will lead you to either success if you get it right or failure if you get it wrong. Even if you find the best investment fund on the planet, if your trend reading is wrong, meaning your timing is wrong, you will fail.

Therefore in your analytical toolkit, you absolutely must have a reliable method to determine future market direction. And if your desire is to become proficient, it is going to take time and patience. Throughout your journey to tax-free riches, you will ideally need to know if you are in a bull (up) market or are you in a bear (down) market.

Key Questions You Have to Ask

But that is not enough. If we are in a bull market, are we in the early stage or the later stage? And more importantly what is the market doing right now? Is it weak and acting badly, or is it merely going through a normal decline (typically 8% to 12%)? This means to win with ISA Trend Investing, you absolutely have to know the state of health that the market is in. Is it healthy (uptrend) meaning it is safe to invest or is it unhealthy (downtrend) meaning you should be out on the sidelines in the safety of cash?

The best way to determine the overall trend and direction of the market is to follow, interpret and understand what the general market averages are doing every day. This is the most important lesson you can learn.

In his bestselling book, *How to Make Money in Stocks*, William O'Neil said: *"Don't let anyone tell you that you can't time the market."*

According to O'Neil, the erroneous belief that no one can time the market evolved more than 30 years ago when most funds that tried it were not successful. This is because they had to buy and sell at exactly the right time but due to their asset size problems, it took weeks to raise cash and weeks to re-enter or get back invested into the market. Therefore, the top management at these funds imposed rules on their fund managers that required them to remain fully invested (95% to 100% of assets).[92]

If you want to make big money in investment funds (or stocks) over the long-term, you must observe and study the major indexes carefully. Here they are:

- The Nasdaq Composite

- The S&P 600

- The S&P 500

- The Dow Jones Industrial Average

As well as watching these four indexes, the action and behaviour of the highest quality stocks (the leaders) is also a key indicator of future market direction.

By studying these four indexes plus the action of leading stocks—each and every day, you will come to realise meaningful changes in the daily behaviour at key turning points like market tops and bottoms and learn how to capitalise on them. As O'Neil explains...

"Recognising when the market has hit a top or has bottomed out is frequently 50% of the whole complicated ballgame."

The buy and hold strategy does not work with ISA Trend Investing. Anybody who was using the buy and hold strategy, and bought a technology fund just before the 2000-2002 bear market, would have probably seen catastrophic losses. And those losses could have been in the region of 75% to 90%. To make up for a loss like that, it can take you as much as a decade or more just to get back to even.

Take a look at this example.

+   A loss of 33% requires a 50% gain just to get back even.

+   A loss of 50% requires a 100% gain just to get back even.

+   A loss of 90% requires a 900% gain just to get back even.

This is why it is so important to preserve your capital and get out of the market and into the safety of a cash based fund when you can see the first signs that the market's health is deteriorating.

Does your current adviser tell you when the market's health is deteriorating?

Do they advise you to switch out of the market at the first signs of a bear market?

Do they suggest that you switch into a cash based fund to protect and preserve your capital?

If they don't, why not?

You see, after you identify the first definite indications of a market top, you can't wait around. You have to quickly get out of your chosen fund/s before real weakness develops. Lightning fast action is critical to ensure you do not give back your hard-earned gains.

Unless you are able to get in and get out of the market at the right time, you will have difficulty making headway. You or your adviser might be able to pick the best fund in the world but unless you get in sync with the market's trend, the fund will not achieve the returns you desire. But if you master the art of determining future market direction, you will have learned **the secret code that can open the vault to unlimited wealth.** Getting in sync with the market is not easy and takes countless hours of practice, taking many years to master. However, knowing the basics about how the market works is going to be of great benefit to you.

It's All about Supply and Demand

Just like the property market, the stock market works on *supply and demand.* Using the property market as an example, house prices, as you know, go up and down in value. Why is it that property prices rise? In a word, demand. Why do they fall? The reason is oversupply. The level of supply and demand is determined by *confidence.*

If there are high levels of confidence and optimism, more people will look to buy. But when confidence is low, people do not want to buy and will therefore be more inclined to sell. When there are more sellers than buyers, prices drop. When people do not want to buy, prices have to drop until they reach a price level where confidence is restored. If houses sell quickly, it means there is demand and this in turn forces up prices. If houses sell slowly, it means that there is no demand or oversupply and that in turn forces prices down. The stock market works in the same way as the property market. It's all based on supply and demand.

It's Time to Get Excited Again

Contrary to popular belief, it is not Joe Public who make up the majority of the market's daily trading volume. As you learned in Chapter 5, it is the professionals that amount to approximately 75% of the trade that goes on—which means these individuals and organisations buy and sell huge amounts of shares.

And because these professionals buy and sell such large volumes of shares, it means that the market's trend and direction is greatly influenced by these big players. And that is why it is best to get in sync with what they are doing.

If the stock market professionals sell, prices drop. If they buy, prices rise. If you try to go against these huge investors and buy when they are selling, you are going to get hurt—and hurt badly. You see, as you've been reminded here on many occasions, three out of every four stocks (and funds) move in the same direction as the market and that is why you have to get in sync with the market's overall trend.

How to Seriously Profit

When the professionals have low confidence about the values in the market, they start to sell. Because they hold such huge amounts of stock, they simply cannot sell all the shares they own in one day. That indicates they have to sell over weeks, months and even years to get completely out of a company they think is overvalued.

Just as with selling, buying into companies takes time too. From this knowledge, <u>you can seriously profit by simply acquiring the ability to read the market's health</u>. If the market is healthy, it will form an uptrend and approximately 75% of stocks and funds will rise with that trend. When it is unhealthy, the trend will be downwards and 75% of stocks and funds will fall.

The multi-million pound question at this stage must be:

How do you read the market's health?

First of all, reading William O'Neil's bestselling, *How to Make Money in Stocks* should ideally be on your things to do list. I always tell my clients to pay particular attention to Chapter 7 entitled "M = Market Direction." In that chapter, you get a simple but detailed explanation of exactly how the market works. And given Bill's great track record, it would be a good use of your time.

In addition to learning from O'Neil, here are some good pointers on how you can get quickly started.

Price and Volume Is Everything

One of the best ways of reading the market is to look at charts. A stock chart is a graph that displays the price and volume history of a given security or index over a period of days, months or even years. Price and volume charts help you to see what the professionals are doing so that you can follow in their footsteps.

Whether they are buying or selling, through a chart you can see what they are doing by simply looking at the *price* and *volume* action. Price action is how a stock or index changes in price. Volume action tells you the number of shares that have been traded.

For example, if volume is far above its average and the price action is up, the professionals are buying. On the other hand, if the volume is far above average and the price action is down, it means that the professionals are selling.

Lack of volume combined with prices moving up indicates little demand from the professionals. This is viewed as unhealthy action.

Lack of volume combined with prices moving down means that the professionals are reluctant to sell. This type of action is viewed as healthy action. By watching the market every day, and keeping a close eye on price and volume action, you can determine exactly what the professionals are doing with their money so that you can do the same.

Price and Volume Action Explained

Below are four images. They show the difference between healthy price and volume action and unhealthy price and volume action.

Healthy Price and Volume Action

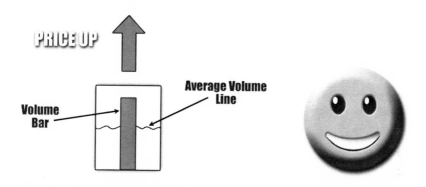

Note: Volume is <u>above</u> average. Price is <u>up</u>

This type of action indicates that the big institutional investors (who control 75% of the 'market's direction') are <u>buying heavy.</u> This is <u>positive.</u>

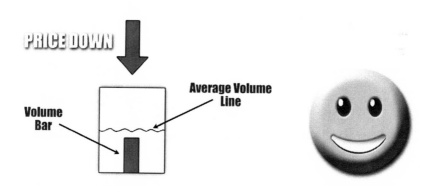

Note: Volume is <u>below</u> average. Price is <u>down</u>

This type of action indicates that the big institutional investors (who control 75% of the 'market's direction') are <u>reluctant</u> to sell. This is <u>positive.</u>

Unhealthy Price and Volume Action

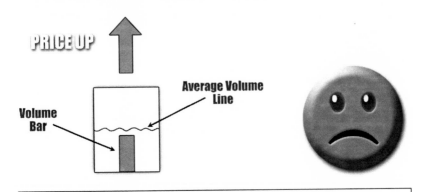

Note: Volume is <u>below</u> average. Price is <u>up</u>

This type of action indicates that the big institutional investors (who control 75% of the 'market's direction') are <u>reluctant</u> to buy. This is <u>negative</u>.

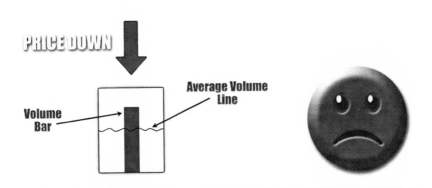

Note: Volume is <u>above</u> average. Price is <u>down</u>

This type of action indicates that the big institutional investors (who control 75% of the 'market's direction') are <u>selling heavy</u>. This is <u>negative</u>.

It is also important for you to understand that it takes a lot of buying or selling to confirm that the trend of the market has changed.

For example, if the trend of the stock market is up, it takes a lot of selling to change the trend from up to down. By measuring how much selling is going on over certain time periods, you can determine when the trend is about to change or has changed and you can then act accordingly ie; switching some of your holding into a cash based fund or completely switching out onto the sidelines.

How to Get on the Inside

Reading the market's health gives you inside knowledge of future market direction and if the market's health has become sickly, it tells you that if you stay invested, your investments have a high probability of dropping in value.

It is helpful to be aware that <u>it's impossible to time getting out at the very top of the market or getting in right at the very bottom</u>. But what you can do, when you know what you are doing, is get in at the first or second floor of the elevator instead of the ground floor. And you can get out not at the very top floor but one or two below it. You therefore only get in or out when a new trend has clearly been established.

Why can't you get out right at the top or in right at the bottom?

The answer is that you only get out of a market after you have seen clear evidence that the professionals have been selling excessive amounts over a short period of time. And when that happens, the market's trend changes and starts to head south. In this example, it is only when the trend change has been confirmed from up to down that you would then make the decision to get out.

Wait for the Confirmation before Committing

At market bottoms, you don't blindly rush in and buy when the market hits a brand new low just because it *feels* right. You see, the market could go even lower. Again you have to wait for a confirmation that the trend has changed from down to up. This can only happen after large amounts of buying from the professionals, again over a short period of time. This proves that it is utter nonsense when people say the market can't be timed. Of course the stock market can be timed, but you do have to know what you are doing—and that knowledge does not come overnight.

That knowledge involves the discipline of reading the market every single day. <u>Face time on the market is what counts</u>. With this in mind, let me ask five important questions. They will help you to determine if your current adviser is helping or hurting you:

Question one. Does your current adviser love the market so much that he or she watches it—in real time—every single day—and even keeps a close eye on it when they go away on holiday?

Question two. Is your current adviser able to read and analyse the price and volume action on stock charts? And know exactly what it means and what appropriate action to take?

Question three. Does your adviser do a thorough two hour analysis on the market after the market has closed for the day?

Question four. Does your current adviser understand how the behaviour of indexes such as the Japanese Nikkei, China's Shanghai Composite and the numerous European market indexes, could influence the direction of the US stock market?

And finally, question five. Does your adviser send you a daily report, or give you a call, to tell you how the market performed for the day and whether or not it is safe to invest—and if it is safe, what he or she is personally investing in so that you can do the same?

The reason these questions are so important is because the market's health and direction can change in a matter of days. Yes, I did say days—and not weeks which means that to win, you need updating daily on what is going on. And if your current adviser does not really understand how the market works, they are probably hurting rather than helping.

Priceless Information about How the Market Works

Observing how the four main indexes are acting is essential to helping you read the market's future trend or direction. However, there are some key indicators that almost every time give you a head start when spotting market turning points—such as market tops and market bottoms. Let me explain.

My philosophy on how the market works is based on numerous factors, rules and principles. One of the things that I like to see happening to confirm that the market is strong and vibrant is the way that the Nasdaq, the Nasdaq 100 and the chip sector are acting.

The Nasdaq 100 includes 100 of the largest domestic and international non-financial securities listed on the Nasdaq market. These include giants such as Microsoft, Google and Cisco Systems. Chips is a common term for semiconductors. The main index for chips is the PHLX Semiconductor SectorSM and is commonly known as the SOX. The SOX is a price-weighted index composed of 18 companies involved in the design, distribution, manufacture, and sale of semiconductors.

If the market is rising but being led by the Dow or the S&P 500, meaning the Nasdaq, the Nasdaq 100 and the chip sector are lagging, this normally means that the rally (uptrend) is more prone to fail. But if the Nasdaq, the Nasdaq 100 and the chip sector are leading the market higher, that tells you the rally is more likely to succeed.

You see, by watching the market every single day, I've noticed that these three key indicators act like a kind of giant magnet. In other words, when they are weak, they tend to pull and lead the market down but when they are strong, they tend to pull and lead the market up. I like to watch the Nasdaq 100's action in two ways. I look at the chart of the Nasdaq 100 and I look at the chart of the QQQQ, which is the exchange-traded fund (ETF) that tracks the movement of the 100.

By watching the QQQQs, I can carefully study the price and volume action of the Nasdaq 100. With chips, I like to watch the SOX and the SMH, which is the exchange-traded fund that tracks the performance of a number of major semiconductor companies. Included in the SMH are Intel, Texas Instruments and Applied Materials. If you are serious about becoming a professional full-time investor, this information I have just shared with you could prove to be priceless. And because these three key indicators give you early signals to act, I watch them very closely and I suggest you do too.

A Common Question Asked by Seekers of Wealth

Some people who haven't read *Liquid Millionaire* ask me this question:

"Please explain why I need to learn about the stock market, its health and its overall trend? Can't I just pick the best investments and then hold them for the long-term?"

When they ask, I explain to them that unless you get the trend and direction right, you are not going to get anything right and you are sure to lose money. I say that, because three out of every four investments (stocks and investment funds) move in the same direction as the market, you must be able to read the market's health and direction or else you are doomed to fail like 90% of investors do.

May I now ask you a question?

Are you fascinated enough about the stock market to put in 10,000 hours to master it?

If you answered yes, that means you can simply follow in my footsteps and do exactly what I did.

<u>Attaining *mastery* in reading the market's health and direction is essential</u>. And you can acquire that mastery by becoming a pro yourself –or by tapping into the mind of a stock market professional.

It is important for you to be aware that your tax-free account is going to eventually grow into six, seven and even eight-figures over the up and coming years. And when your account suddenly drops in value, you will need to know whether the fall is a healthy one or whether the drop is leading to something more serious. When your portfolio loses value, which it will, even when the market is in an uptrend, you are going to need to be *certain* whether the drop is healthy or unhealthy. You have to know whether to sit out the correction or whether you should be "parked" in cash on the sidelines.

Mastery Is the Key

Without the confidence that comes with knowing your stuff, you are more likely to make the wrong decision and end up possibly losing a lot of money. When the market does drop and you know with certainty that something is wrong, that is when you can get out of the market and get out fast.

Of course knowing with absolute conviction whether the market is in trouble or not can only be achieved when you have attained market trend mastery. <u>As your capital builds up, the need for understanding market direction (health) becomes even more important</u>. If you try to follow your gut instincts, you are going to experience plenty of pain, so please be careful.

Edwin Lefevre, author of the classic *Reminiscences of a Stock Operator*, once said, *"In a bear market all stocks go down and in a bull market they go up."*

The people who failed to get out of previous bear markets such as 2000-2002 and the one that began Oct 2007 will have probably lost anywhere between 50% to 80% of their portfolio's value.

And imagine if you took an 80% loss just two years before you were planning to retire?

The scary thing is that a portfolio valued at one million pounds would reduce down to just £200,000. I am sure you will agree that that sort of damage would probably cause some serious financial and emotional pain.

As a reminder, an 80% loss on your portfolio needs a 400% move to the upside just to get back even.

How long would that take?

Awareness Can Make You Rich

When the market takes a heavy fall, investors who do not know how the market works will blame either the fund manager or their advisers for their losses. But what they really should be doing is noticing and understanding the link between their fund value dropping and the market heading downwards.

You see, most investors do not know that three out of four stocks will always move in the same direction as the market. If they realised this basic law of how the market works, they would be able to switch their thinking from blaming to learning. And if they did learn how the market works, they'd then be able to act swiftly when the market was showing signs that it was unhealthy and quickly switch into the safety of cash to help protect and preserve their hard earned money.

Know More about How the Market Works Than 95% of IFA's

Okay, with what you have just learned, you now know more about how the market works than 95% of accountants, bank managers, stock brokers, financial advisers and stock market investors.

That is why so many people find the information in this book so valuable, especially when they use it to profit.

But does reading the market in this way really work?

And does it work in both bullish (up) and bearish (down) market environments?

As I have said before, this timing system that I use is not flawless but it does tend to get it right about 80-90% of the time. As you are aware, it helped me to correctly time the beginning *and* the end of the 2003-2007 bull market. This is the one that officially started in March 2003 and ended Oct 2007.

On a few occasions in this book, I have talked about how timing the upside has paid off for me and my clients, but what about the downside?

As a rule, most people are interested in how they can *make* money in the stock market, but many of my clients are just as interested in *protecting* their wealth. After all, many of them come to us when they have already built up quite substantial cash holdings. Many of my clients were pretty pleased with themselves in 2004.

A System That Helps Protect and Preserve Your Profits

As you are aware, the system that my clients and I use has a goal of beating the Nasdaq. And in 2004, the Nasdaq closed the year up 8.6% whereas the system we use closed the year up 32.5%.[93] But the one thing that really impressed my clients the most with regards to that 32.5% one year gain was the fact that during 2004, the Nasdaq had a massive 19% correction. And yet the system still managed to avoid it and score such a healthy gain.

Another example of the system being able to accurately time the market on the downside came in early 2007. As I have said previously, the timing system I use will not get you out right at the market peak nor will it get you in right at the bottom.

And as American financier and stock market speculator Bernard Baruch famously said, *"Don't try to buy at the bottom or sell at the top. This can't be done—except by liars."*

On 28th February 2007, my clients and I exited the market. The market was showing definite signs that something was wrong.

The market was telling me that the trend had changed from an uptrend to a downtrend. Because of this change, we were forced to switch our tax-free holdings into the safety of a cash based fund. After switching out, the market then proceeded to go lower but eventually started to rebound. Over the next 8 months, the market saw rises on low volume (indicating a lack of demand) followed by falls on heavy volume (indicating professional selling) further confirming all was not well. This action kept me, my brother, our team and our clients out of the market because it was clear to me that it was not safe to invest.

Predicting the End of the 2003-2007 Bull Market

Even though the market did form another uptrend over this 8 month period, it was not a market where you could make money. Let me explain. Every time the market gained ground, it quickly turned tail and came crashing down. It really was a horrible market environment and it felt really good to be out on the sidelines. On 31st October 2007, the market finally and officially topped out. It then proceeded to hurtle south and the falls were sharp, fast and brutal. The Nasdaq bear market was made official (20% or more off a recent high) on 22nd January 2008.

But what is interesting to note is that the type of funds you have seen throughout this book tend to drop *more* than the Nasdaq when the general market is falling. This indicates that staying invested in such a fund when the market is unhealthy is a strategy for amateur investors.

For example, look at what happened to this fund that HIRE CAR™ found. We were fortunate to exit this fund the day after it topped, but anybody who played the buy and hold game with this one would be seriously licking their wounds.

● Fund: Legg Mason Japan Equity Fund - Acc
● Index: Select index

Analysis of the Legg Mason Japan Equity Fund A ACC as it happened

1. Buy Point (Bought@2.515. on 17/06/05)

2. On the 17/01/06 the fund drops - 8.1% - ISACO places sell order
    (Sell price @ 3.323 – **Profit Made +30.5% in 6 Months**)

3. On the 08/02/08 when chart was taken the price was 1.052. The fund is
    now – 68.31% off its high.

Important Note: A Buy & Hold strategy would have resulted in a loss of -58.76%

Data Supplied by Morningstar.

In other words, a typical fund will correct as much as 1½ to 2 times–or even more–when the market is in a downtrend.[94] So if the market falls 25%, expect investment funds to possibly fall 33%-50%–or even more.

Taking a hit like that on your portfolio is going to be like getting a punch in the stomach.

Plus it is going to take you a long time to get that money back.

Remember what you learned earlier.

- A loss of 33% requires a 50% gain just to get back even.

- A loss of 50% requires a 100% gain just to get back even.

- A loss of 90% requires a 900% gain just to get back even.

This is why you have to get your timing right or your portfolio could end up in a real mess. If you try to swim against the current, it will literally leave you gasping for air. And some of my clients who have seven figure plus portfolios were very happy about the fact that if they hadn't followed my lead during 2007 and early 2008, their portfolios could have seen losses as large as £500,000 or maybe more.

Remember This and You Won't Go Far Wrong

To close this chapter, let me say this. How the market *really* works is not my opinion.

As Jesse Livermore once wrote, *"Markets are never wrong—opinions often are."*

How the market works is how the market has worked since it began in the late 1800's. It is always about supply and demand and the way to analyse supply and demand is through looking at price and volume action on stock charts.

But many people are not aware of that key fact. When they ask for my opinion on what is going on with the market, I always give them the facts based on <u>what the market has been doing</u>. But unfortunately some people get sucked into the media headlines and mistakenly think that the facts I am sharing with them are totally wrong. For example, let's say that the market has been acting really well and all the signs are showing that the institutional investors are seriously buying stocks.

That is a bullish indicator and tells you that the market is more likely to head north than sideways or south. But the news on TV, radio and in the newspapers at this time may be mentioning things such as "terrorism," "war," "recession," "bear market" and any other forms of negativity. The best investors in the world never get sucked into the pessimism of the media and always instead look at the facts. I tell you all this because there are going to be times from this point onwards–where the market is telling you that all is well but the majority of people are saying the opposite.

Stay Away from Know-It-Alls

When I tell people that the market has been acting well–even though the news headlines say the opposite–it never surprises me when a person decides to challenge my market outlook. This challenger nearly always turns out to be a know-it-all who is totally fixed in their thinking.

This person might say something like, *"But what about the price of oil?"* or *"A recession is looming and that's going to affect the market,"* or *"The dollar is putting serious pressure on sterling right now."* But every time I hear this type of talk, I always refer them back to supply and demand and remind them about price and volume action.

I say to them, these are the facts. The facts say that right now all is well. I also remind them that I cannot predict into the future. But what I can do is to tell them what is happening right now and where the market is likely to head in the immediate term. Things can quickly change and the professionals from time to time alter their stance based upon new information. How this news will affect the market and stocks is constantly being fed to these professionals hour by hour and minute by minute.

How to Read the Market Like a True Pro

In other words, the big institutional investors can be bullish one minute but then discover some new information that overrides their optimistic outlook. At the end of the day, to effectively read the market like a true pro, you have to remember that it really does not matter what is happening news wise. Irrelevant of what the news or any market commentator is saying, if the price and volume is positive, then that's good, period.

And that goes for the downside too. If all the headlines are positive but price and volume are saying the opposite, then you had better be thinking about switching into the safety of cash. The lesson here is simple. Do not let the news tell you what is going on or going to happen. Instead, look at what is really going on by studying the price and volume action on charts. But if you are pushed for time and have no inclination to become a proficient chart reader, get help from a professional with a great track record. Look for a person with integrity, a person who you trust and who matches your values. Do this and you won't go far wrong.

It is now time to move on, my friend.

One million pounds in liquid is a lot of money to many people, but would you be interested in how your first liquid million could turn into £75 million…tax-free?

You would?

That tells me you are probably going to love this next chapter.

Here is a great way of…

CHAPTER 8

Turning Your First Million into £75 Million

"Compound interest"
– Albert Einstein's reply when asked to
name man's greatest invention.

If you acquire the skill of being able to get your money to grow at 20%–which of course is not going to be easy, but it is possible–your first million could end up turning into a £75 million pound fortune–or even more.

How is this possible?

By making it a goal to become a centenarian (a person who is 100 or over), using ISA Trend Investing, it could help to make you worth a staggering £75 million.

Does this sound too good to be true? Let me explain.

Because the ISA wrapper stays with you for life, if you follow the 7% Withdrawal Formula, your tax-free pot is going to grow into a huge sum.

7% Withdrawal Formula

When you arrive at your intended financial tax-free goal, you simply follow the steps below.

Step 1 - You withdraw *just enough* money to pay for your dream lifestyle.

Step 2 - You then continue to grow what is left in your tax-free pot for another year.

Step 3 - You simply repeat this process each year for the rest of your life.

Can it be that simple?

Yes.

When you get this 3 step process right, your lifestyle each year gets better and you get richer. But, if you mess with the formula, things can and will go horribly wrong. The lesson is, stick to the formula or you could live to regret it. Let me explain the right way to do it by using an example.

How to Become Richer Each and Every Year

You and your partner set a goal to make £1 million pounds by the time you are 60, using ISAs. After reaching your target, you then set up an automatic 7% withdrawal which in turn would help to fund your lifestyle. Now, if you master the skill of growing your money at 20% per year, your large chunk of capital, after your lifestyle costs have been taken out, will continue to grow at approximately 11.6% every year.

To put it another way, you become richer each year. Because you and your partner accumulated £1 million pounds, you would then withdraw £70,000 (7% of £1 million) to pay for your lifestyle. Your million would drop to £930,000 and then grow at a rate of 20%. At the end of the year, you would have £1,116,000. This means that even though you have taken money out to pay for your lifestyle, your original £1 million pounds has grown by 11.6%.

The following year's 7% of cash flow would be £78,120. This equates to an 11.6% increase from the previous year's living expenses. As you can see, the great thing is that if you follow the 7% formula and manage to get your money to grow at 20% each year, your main lump sum gets bigger, making you richer each year *and* your lifestyle even better.

And if we stick with this example, you can clearly see what happens as you get older:

At age 70, you'd have £195,000 cash flow to pay for your lifestyle and a tax-free fortune of £2.79 million.

At age 80, you would have £584,000 cash flow and a tax-free fortune of £8.35 million.

At age 90, you'd have £1.75 million cash flow and a tax-free fortune of £25 million.

And if you managed to hit the magic 100 mark, you would have £5.25 million cash flow and a tax-free fortune of £75 million pounds!

Coco Chanel once said, *"There are people who have money and people who are rich."*

What you have just seen is the power of compound interest going to work on your behalf. It is mind boggling, isn't it? The thing that most people say at this point is something along the lines of:-

"But even if I did make it to 100, I would be too old to enjoy it."

And I reply…Nonsense.

You see, I have a strong belief that human beings, if we wanted to, could live far longer lives–if only we decided to learn *how*. I have a conviction that I will live until I am at least 100…and I'm not joking. Let me share with you why I have this concrete belief.

The Universal Law of Cause and Effect

What makes the whole concept of achieving your financial dream more exciting is that we all seem to have a relatively high level of control over what age we are going to live to. It is all about *cause and effect* or as some people put it, sowing and reaping.[95] This means that if we are smart and make a decision that we are going to live a very long life, you can not only enjoy the journey, you can also relish the many decades that follow after you hit your main target.

I really do believe that we can almost choose how long we want to live. I say this because every single one of us has the power of choice. We can decide how we want to live. I know that this is common sense but it is good to remind ourselves that on the one hand a person can choose to take good care of themselves by eating the right foods, exercising regularly, resting as appropriate etc–or they can choose to neglect their bodies. One course of action will help and the other will hurt.

As Brian Tracy states; *"Everything counts."*

If a person can start to think longer term they would probably start to make better decisions in the present.

Have you decided how long you want to live for?

How to Increase Your Life Expectancy

As you've probably gathered, I am a very big believer in the laws of probability and although it is hard to guarantee things one hundred percent, I think that all of us can put the odds of success on our side if we want to. This leads us very nicely into the subject of life expectancy. Many articles nowadays are telling us that we are living longer. When you see these write-ups in the newspaper, even though I see living longer as a positive, the media almost always seem to put a negative slant on it, stating that because we are living longer, people don't and won't have enough cash to cope. Living longer and not having enough money could therefore cause a lot of pain.

That future pain of course could be avoided by some simple financial planning. The positive side to everybody living longer is the fact that when you get your finances in order, you can then enjoy the lifestyle that you have worked so hard to create. I recently did some research on life expectancy and discovered that in 1900, it was only 47.[96]

More recent data from the continuous mortality investigation shows the annual increase in life expectancy of a 65 year old male from 1985 to 2005 was 2%.[97] The statistics showed that the life expectancy of a man, aged 65, living in the UK in 1985 was 78.8 years of age. But in 2005, the life expectancy had jumped to 84.4 years of age.

What would happen if this trend continues?

A person aged 39 in 2008 may expect to live until he or she is almost 100. And that is if he or she just met the average!

This means making better choices in the now–based on long-term thinking–could help a person to live far and above the 100 mark.

Let's take a case study to explain what I am getting at.

I am going to use my gran, Ivy Sutherland as an example. Ivy was born in 1915, which tells you that in 2008, when she very peacefully passed on, she was 93. In the year she was born, life expectancy was just 54.[98] When my gran was born, there is no way that her parents would have believed that she was going to live past 90, as that would have been 66.7% more than the life expectancy prediction.

It would be like saying that a child born today is going to live until they are 143. People just would not be able to get their heads around it. Can you imagine somebody telling my gran's parents that she was going to live past 90 when at that time life expectancy was 54? People would think that they were crazy to make such a claim. Now let's move on a little in time. By the time Gran was 35 (in 1950) life expectancy for women had risen to 71.[99]

Be Careful About What People Tell You

Had Gran listened to and *believed* the life expectancy statistics of 1950 (when she was 35) she may, because of the power of belief, have passed on around 1986 instead of in 2008, 22 years later. One reason why we should not pay too much attention to the current life expectancy figures is because if we set in our minds on a certain age that we believe we are going to live to, we might pop our clogs prematurely–simply because we believe that the end is near.

Let me give you some examples of how the power of belief can have potentially negative effects.

The first examples are taken from Dr Denis Waitley's excellent *The Psychology of Winning*.[100]

"...a young aborigine who, during a journey, slept at an older friend's home. For breakfast, the friend had prepared a meal consisting of wild hen, a food which the young were strictly prohibited from eating. The young man demanded to know whether the meal consisted of wild hen and the host responded 'No.' The young man then ate the meal and departed. Several years later, when the two friends met again, the older man asked his friend whether he would now eat a wild hen. The young man said he would not since he had been solemnly ordered not to do so by his elder tribesman. The older man laughed and told him how he had been previously tricked into eating this forbidden food. The young man became extremely frightened and started to tremble. Within twenty-four hours he was dead!

In the Western world, many equivalents to voodoo death have been discovered in case histories.

'You will die,' the fortune teller predicted, 'when you are 43.'

That prediction was made 38 years before when the fortune teller's client was 5 years old. The little girl grew up with the awesome prediction on her mind—and died one week after her 43rd birthday, said a report in the British Medical Journal.

'We wonder if the severe emotional tensions of this patient superimposed on the physiological stress of surgery had any bearing upon her death,' the doctors said.

They suggested she may have been frightened to death and said the case was that of an apparently healthy woman, a mother of five, who underwent a relatively minor operation. Two days later she was dead.

The doctors said that the night before the woman confessed to her sister—who knew of the fortune telling incident—that she did not expect to awaken from the anaesthesia. On the morning of the operation, the woman told a nurse she was certain she was going to die. An hour after the operation she collapsed and lost consciousness. A post mortem revealed extensive internal bleeding for which there was no reasonable explanation. A spokesman from the British Medical Association said, 'There is no medical *explanation to account for this. It seems rather like the case of natives who die on the date and at the time the witch doctor predicts.'*

Consider, also the death of Elvis Presley, the rock-star legend. He also died shortly before his 43rd birthday, of the same cause, at the same age, as did his mother. And he expected it to happen!"

This next story also illustrates the negative impacts that the power of belief can have on a person's health and life span. It was taken from Maxwell Malz's *The New Psycho-Cybernetics.*[101]

Just like in the first example taken from Denis Waitley's book, this one involves voodoo. Personally I think it is a remarkable story of how a false belief aged a man twenty years.

Briefly, the story is this: Maltz, a plastic surgeon, performed a cosmetic operation on Mr Russell's lower lip for a very modest fee, under the condition that he must tell his girlfriend that the operation had cost him his entire life savings. Her reaction was not as Mr Russell had anticipated. She became hysterically angry and called him a fool for having spent all his money. In her anger and disgust she announced that she was placing a voodoo curse on him. Both Mr Russell and his girlfriend had been born on an island in the West Indies where voodoo was practiced by the ignorant and superstitious.

When in the heat of anger, his girlfriend "cursed" him, Mr Russell felt vaguely uncomfortable but did not think much about it. However, he remembered and wondered when a short time later he felt a strange small hard bump on the inside of his lip. A friend who knew of the voodoo curse, insisted that he see a Dr. Smith, who promptly assured him that the bump inside his mouth was the feared African Bug, which would slowly eat away all his vitality and strength. Mr Russell began to worry and look for signs of waning strength. He wasn't long in finding them. He lost his appetite and his ability to sleep.

Maltz learned all this from Mr Russell when he returned to his office several weeks after he had dismissed him. Maltz's nurse did not recognise him and no wonder. The Mr Russell who had originally called upon Dr Maltz had been a very impressive individual. He stood six feet four, a large man with the physique of an athlete and the bearing and manner that bespoke an inner dignity and gave him a magnetic personality.

The Mr Russell who now sat across the desk of Maltz had aged at least twenty years. His hands shook with the tremor of age. His eyes and cheeks were sunken. He had lost perhaps thirty pounds. The changes in his appearance were all characteristic of the process that medical science, for want of a better name, calls aging.

After a quick examination of his mouth, Dr Maltz assured Mr Russell that he could get rid of the African Bug in less than 30 minutes, which he did. The bump which had caused all the trouble was merely a small bit of scar tissue from his operation. Maltz removed it, held it in his hand and showed it to Russell. Maltz states: "The important thing is he saw the truth and believed it."

Mr Russell gave a sigh of relief, and it seemed as if there was almost an immediate change in his posture and expression. Several weeks later, Dr Maltz received a nice letter from Mr Russell with a photograph of him and his new bride. He had gone back to his home and married his childhood sweetheart. The man in the picture was the original Mr Russell. He had grown young again overnight. A false belief had aged him twenty years. The truth had not only set him free from fear and restored his confidence, but had actually reversed the aging process.

And so, with these stories in mind, when people are told by doctors they only have a certain amount of time to live, by the power of belief, that prediction often becomes reality.

Author of the excellent *The Magic of Believing*, Claude M. Bristol once wrote, *"Our fear thoughts are just as creative or just as magnetic in attracting troubles to us as are the constructive and positive thoughts in attracting positive results."*

It is also interesting to know that there are stories of people who have fought the doctors' doom and gloom predictions, refusing to believe their negative prognoses. And sometimes we see examples of people who defied the beliefs of these men in white jackets and lived much longer than the doctor in question had originally predicted.

And so it might be a good idea for us all to be careful about the input we receive and what we decide to believe.

As Henry Ford famously said, *"Whether you believe you can do a thing or not, you are right."*

Another example of false life expectancies comes in the example of the late George Burns. George was an Academy Award-winning American comedian, actor and writer. He was born in 1896, when life expectancy was just 49. George lived until he was 100, meaning he doubled his life expectancy figure.

Believing that you are going to live way past the century mark is a great belief to adopt, don't you think?

Life Extension—How It Will Positively Affect Our World

Are you ready to push your beliefs a little further?

I hope so, because during my research on life expectancy, I came across some very interesting data on the subject of life extension. Ray Kurzweil and Dr Aubrey de Grey are known authorities on this subject. They both have a solid belief that we are very close to discovering how we as humans can live forever. Yes, I did say forever. Immortality—would that interest you?

Woody Allen had this to say on the subject: *"I don't want to achieve immortality through my work. I want to achieve immortality through not dying."*

Immortality is a very contentious subject, I know, but if you have an open mind, Kurzweil and Aubrey de Grey are worth checking out.

You Could Live Way Past the Century Mark

If you want to be blown away, read Dr Aubrey de Grey's thinking. This was taken from an article found on www.livescience.com. The article was posted 11 April 2005, and starts with the interviewer Ken Than making the following comments to summarise a recent interview with the formidable Dr de Grey.

"Time may indeed be on your side—if you can just last another quarter century.

By then, people will start lives that could last 1,000 years or more. Our human genomes will be modified to include the genetic material of micro-organisms that live in the soil, enabling us to break down the junk proteins that our cells amass over time and which they can't digest on their own.

People will have the option of looking and feeling the way they did at 20 for the rest of their lives, or opt for an older look if they get bored.

Of course, everyone will be required to go in for age rejuvenation therapy once every decade or so, but that will be a small price to pay for near-immortality. This may sound like science fiction, but Aubrey de Grey thinks this could be our reality in as little as 25 years. Other scientists caution that it is far from clear whether and for how long science can stall the inevitable.

De Grey, a Cambridge University researcher, heads the Strategies for Engineered Negligible Senescence (SENS) project, in which he has defined seven causes of aging, all of which he thinks can be dealt with. (Senescence is scientific jargon for aging.)"

Do You Have an Ultimate Goal in Life?

While you ponder on what you have just read, we can now move on to what I consider another big part of living longer and at the same time maximizing your probability of financial success.

I like to refer to it as your *Ultimate Goal in Life*.

My brother Paul and I learned that if you want to live and experience an extraordinary life, it is a wise idea to have a big challenging life goal, something that you are intensely passionate about, a goal that fills you with excitement.

Apparently, the best ultimate goals are ones that get you to stretch and grow into the person you are truly capable of becoming. This ultimate goal is what bestselling author Napoleon Hill referred to as your *Major Definite Purpose*.

To help a person attain true peace of mind, their ultimate goal ideally needs to be a double win situation.

Here is a personal example to explain exactly what I mean.

Stephen and Paul's Ultimate Goal

Our ultimate goal is to build a foundation that provides Super Schools for deserving individuals.

The schools will provide world-class education.

The schools are unique. The education taught is a combination of traditional subjects and ones which are not normally covered by the current school curriculum. We will refer to these subjects as life skills.

The life skills taught cover subjects such as "Cognitive Psychology", "The Self Concept, The Self Ideal and The Self Image", "The Power of the Subconscious Mind", "Choice Theory", "Success", "How to Win in Life", "Thinking", "How to Negotiate", "Achievement", "Accelerated Learning Techniques", "Leadership", "Goal Setting", "How to Increase Your Confidence and Self-Esteem", "Happiness", "Wealth Building", "Influence and Persuasion", "Sales and Marketing", "Secrets to Effective Communication", "Problem Solving", "Health, Wellbeing and Life Extension", "Multiple Intelligences" and "Business-Building."

The goal of the school is to produce leaders, experts and authorities in every conceivable field known to man. This in turn helps to make a huge contribution to our planet.

So there you have it. That is our Ultimate Goal.

Do you like the idea of having an Ultimate Goal in Life?

If you do, what is yours going to be?

I sincerely hope that one day you will share it with me. Maybe you will tell me all about it aboard your yacht or maybe whilst flying on your private jet?

Now it is time to move on, my friend.

In the next chapter, you are going to learn all about The Ultimate Wealth Building Model.

And…we are also going to explore some frequently asked questions such as:

"What steps should you take if you want to become a full-time professional investor?"

"What happens if you do not make enough money to help you Retire Rich in ten years?"

And finally…"Are there ways you could significantly increase your income? And if yes, how?"

If you would like to know the answer to questions such as these, this next and final chapter might be just what you have been waiting for.

Get ready. It is time for you to learn how you can profit from...

CHAPTER 9

The Ultimate Wealth Building Model

"Formal education will make you a living;
self-education will make you a fortune."
– Jim Rohn

Before sharing with you The Ultimate Wealth Building Model, I did promise in an earlier chapter I would share with you a step by step plan for the Do It Yourself route. If you remember, this is the path you would take if your goal is to become a full-time professional stock market investor.

If you are really serious about going down the DIY route, I suggest you use what you discover here and combine it with what you learned in Chapter 1. This will enable you to create a master plan. This plan should include how you are going to make the transfer from what you are doing now into becoming a full-time stock market professional investor.

Whenever making the transfer from one career to another, people usually put it off because of fear. This fear is normally caused by the prospect of the unknown. What if it doesn't work out? - What if I fail? - What will people say? These are just some of the doubts that enter into our minds when we are considering making a big change in our life.

A concern for most people is when they realise that if they did pack in their job, they would no longer have an income coming in each and every month.

The solution is simple. Keep your job, start working on your plan and start investing in your spare time such as evenings and weekends. Before you consider dropping your present career to move into a full-time investor's role, make sure that you have at least 6 month's living expenses to fall back on just in case.

And with your plan, I suggest that the time span be at least 3-5 years.

The Do It Yourself Route

- Create a master plan. Your plan should include the following objectives.

  Objective 1: To become highly proficient in reading the trend of the market.

Objective 2: To create and develop a winning system to find quality investment funds.

Objective 3: To create and develop a winning system to find quality stocks.

- Your two systems; one for helping you to find funds and one for helping you find stocks; need to include *rules* and *guidelines* such as selection, when to buy and when to sell.

- To help with creating your system to find the best investment funds, get extremely familiar with investment fund database websites such as www.morningstar.co.uk and www.trustnet. co.uk. Note: It was studying the funds listed on Morningstar that helped me to develop HIRE CAR™. HIRE CAR™ is far from a perfect system and everything can be improved. If a school thicko like me, with a grade F in maths, can create a system for finding funds, then so can you.

- Remember that the most important thing when finding a winning fund is the fund manager. The manager's past performance is everything.

- To help with becoming highly proficient in reading the trend of the market, include in your plan reading Chapter 7 in this book over and over again. To help with objectives 1 and 3, read all the books William O'Neil has written and all the books O'Neil has read.[102] He mentions all the books he has read in his own books and audio programs. Do this at your own pace. To help with this task, I have highlighted them in **bold** in the recommended reading section in Appendix B, which can be found at the back of this book.

- With your stock trading, set up an account that allows you to trade US stocks and at low trading charges (for example, $10 per trade / £5 per trade).[103]

- If you can afford it, subscribe to O'Neil's equity research package (this is the one I subscribe to) which costs $1000 per year.[104] The package you opt for needs to include both *Daily Graphs*™ and *Daily Graphs Industry Groups*™. After subscribing, learn how to use the package to find stocks and discover where the big money is flowing, especially when the market is heating up.

- Start to read O'Neil's daily column; The Big Picture every day. You will find it on www.investors.com (you have to be a subscriber to get access to it).

- Have a look at all the other things O'Neil has on his site to continually immerse yourself in the CAN SLIM™ system.

- When you believe the market is healthy, look for potential stocks to buy.

- Paper trade one stock that you get really excited about. DO NOT use real money at this stage. This is where you need to prove to yourself that you can do it. As mentioned in Chapter 1, paper trading is simulated trading that investors use to practice mimicking trades (buys and sells) without actually entering into any monetary transactions. Paper trading is a good way to learn the ropes without risking any money. You can do it simply by pretending to buy and sell stock and keep notes of paper profits or losses.

- I suggest you successfully paper trade a total of 5-10 stocks before using real money.

- Analyse each trade. What did you do right? Why did you get it right? Where did you go wrong? Why? Keep a journal of your trades, thought processes and decisions.

- When you start real money trading, use a maximum of £100 per trade. Do this even if you feel you can afford to trade much higher amounts. This is the time you will be honing your skill before you start to commit larger amounts.

- Buy one stock at a time. Do not be tempted to buy more than one until you get consistent results.

- Create good habits of discipline such as cutting losses quickly, not buying extended stocks, not investing when the market is unhealthy, not investing too much money, analysing every trade, accounting for all your money and documenting your returns versus the Nasdaq.

- On your first trades, your £ losses should be no more than £8 per trade (ie; 8% of £100).

- Analyse all your trades and learn from them.

- Aim to get consistency and solid returns before upping your stakes / buying more than one stock at a time.

- Always look at the downside of every trade you do. Ask, *what is the maximum I would lose if this trade goes against me?* If you can't handle the loss, do not place it, or lower the amount you are about to invest.

- Consider at some point going over to America to see William O'Neil in seminar.[105] Aim to eventually attend his advanced course.[106]

- Keep going and never stop learning. Remember that patience will be needed because it may take 3-5 years of hard graft before you start seeing the results you desire.

- If you keep going and keep learning from your mistakes and course correcting, by default you will end up becoming a professional investor.

Okay, so now you know what to do if you want to take the DIY route. This is the same road that I went down. But remember, only take this route if you are passionate about the market, want to become a professional investor, are prepared to put in at least 10,000 hours of study and you would do it even if you weren't getting paid.

Let's now move on to a different scenario.

What if you read this book, get really excited, have no desire to become a professional stock market investor and instead you want to get our help....but you have one slight snag; you simply do not have the capital required to become one of my clients?

Well here is the answer:

1) Read and apply what you learn in the Special Wealth Building Report (BONUS section, page xxv) that details: How to Increase Your Income x 10 over the Next 3 ½ Years.

2) Start right now to make yourself more valuable to the market place. The best way to do this is to focus on significantly increasing your income. You do this by continually increasing your knowledge and skills.

As scientist, inventor, statesman, and philosopher Benjamin Franklin famously said, *"An investment in knowledge always pays the best interest."*

Some people ask me, should I put all my eggs in one basket? Should I put everything into the stock market?

This is how I respond:

I first remind them of the four things that determine how much money they will make over any given period of time.

THE PERFORMANCE QUADRANT

INTERNAL
(in your control)

EXTERNAL
(out of your control)

INVESTMENT VEHICLE

MARKET DIRECTION

MARKET TIMING

MARKET STRENGTH

I then say to them:

Now let's imagine that you have a goal to become a multi-millionaire in the next ten years or less. Let's also imagine that all your eggs are in the stock market basket. This means you are fully reliant on the stock market making a decent move over the next decade.

The question is, what if the market does not make the move?

They then realise that putting all their eggs in one basket carries far too much risk. They then say, so what should I do?

This is my reply:

Think of your wealth like a cake. Now split that cake into thirds.

Approximately one third of your wealth can be invested into the stock market (for example, ISA and SIPP Trend Investing), another third can be invested into property and the final third can be in self. The key to getting to your goal on time, lowering the risk and maximising your probability of success is to look at what is in your control and look at what is out of your control. Not only is the stock market direction out of your control, so is the property market.

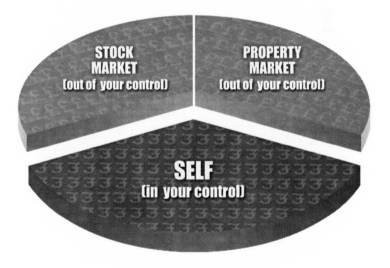

... and that should send you a strong message that the property market should not be relied upon to get you to your goal by a certain time. Again, just like the stock market, property moves in trends and that means you need patience.

With an investment in self, things are a little different.

Self = Earning Power, or how much you are currently worth to the market place.

This is based on a virtually limitless sliding scale. For example, the two founders of Google, Larry Page and Serge Brin, were recently quoted to be earning a million dollars per hour![107] Therefore, the more in-demand you are, the more you are financially worth. In other words, **your earning ability is the one thing you have total control over.** If you want to increase what you earn, simply make yourself more valuable.

When you make yourself indispensable you can choose the team you want to work on, which gives you a very high probability of producing income even if the overall economy is in a bad way.

In a nutshell:

The best thing to focus on—when it comes to having 100% control over how much money you make—is yourself. Whether you decide to become an entrepreneur or you go down the route of climbing the corporate ladder, the key is to ADD VALUE.

Einstein said, *"Try not to become a man of success, but rather try to become a man of value."*

Therefore, if you want to almost guarantee that you will get to your goal of becoming liquid rich in 10 years or less, your main focus should be to invest in yourself and continually upgrade your skills and knowledge so that you become more valuable, needed, in demand and virtually indispensable. Doing this helps you to earn more money and when you earn more, it is easier to save and invest larger amounts. And when you save and invest larger and larger amounts each and every year, it increases the probability of you succeeding enormously.

Reading and Learning Helps You to Think and Feel Better

But working on yourself by reading books, listening to audio programs and attending seminars is not just about increasing your value to the market place. Learning more helps you to become more aware. It not only helps you to *think* better, it helps you to *feel* better too. This is a much greater benefit.

When I was reading Jim Rohn's fabulous book; *The Five Major Pieces to the Life Puzzle*, I read a section in the book that made a big impact on my thinking about why it is that most people don't feel too good about their lives—and why most people fail to produce the results they desire:

"If we were to ask some people why they feel the way they do about certain issues, we would probably discover that the reason why they feel the way they do is because they don't really know a great deal about those issues. Lacking all the information, they form conclusions based on the bits and pieces that have come their way. With their limited knowledge, they often make poor decisions about how things are. If they knew better, they would think better. In other words, they would reach better conclusions simply by increasing their knowledge.

And here is another part of the equation: If they knew better, they would feel better. Why would they feel better? Because they would begin to make better decisions, they would start making better choices, which would produce better results."

What this profound passage tells you is that if only people would increase their knowledge, they would be able to live and experience a better quality of life.

How to Take the Risk Out of Your Financial Future

In Brian Tracy's outstanding book *Maximum Achievement*, he says that when it comes to Financial Freedom you owe it to yourself to develop your own unique talents and abilities to the point where you know that you can *earn* enough money so that you do not have to worry about it:

"The fourth ingredient of success is financial freedom. To be financially free means that you have enough money so that you don't worry about it continually, as most people do. It is not money that lies at the root of all evil; it is the lack of money. Achieving

your own financial freedom is one of the most important goals and responsibilities for your life. It is far too important to be left to chance.

Fully 80 percent of the population are preoccupied with money problems. They think about and worry about money when they wake up in the morning, while they're having breakfast, and throughout the day. They talk about it during the evening. This is not a happy, healthy way to live. This is not conducive to being the best you can be.

Money is important. While I put it as number four on the list of ingredients for success, it is an essential factor in the achievement of the first three. Most worry, stress, anxiety and lost peace of mind are caused by money worries. Many health problems are caused by stress and worry about money. Many problems in relationships are caused by money worries, and one of the main causes of divorce is arguments over money. You therefore owe it to yourself to develop your talents and abilities to the point where you know that you can earn enough money so that you don't have to worry about it."

How to Guarantee You Will Make It

Would you like to know how to literally guarantee that one day you will achieve Financial Freedom and retire liquid rich?

Guaranteeing Financial Freedom starts with making the decision in advance that you will never give up no matter what. You see, <u>as long as you refuse to quit, you must eventually be successful</u>. The longer you persist, the more convinced and determined you become. You finally reach the point where nothing can stop you. And nothing will.

Here is a good question for you. What would a person do if the deadline for their financial goal was ten years and they didn't make it in time?

Once again the answer is simple:-

Keep going–Never stop–Never give in.

Napoleon Hill once said, *"Persistence is to the character of man as carbon is to steel."*

There is one trait that will almost guarantee a person will succeed in their quest for riches and that trait is persistence. People who develop an attitude of, "I will never quit and would rather die than give up on my goal," have the right mindset to achieve phenomenal financial success. To be persistent, a person has to develop total self-belief.

And as Albert Bandura once wrote, *"Self-belief does not necessarily ensure success but self-disbelief assuredly spawns failure."*

It seems like it might be a good idea then to make it a habit to act courageously when it is called upon.

When a person is following a proven strategy and they have total belief in themselves, they automatically exercise courage and start to make persistence a deeply ingrained habit.

The Winning Attitude

Having an, I will never, ever give up on my goal, type of attitude is going to help you sail through the rough seas that come as part and parcel of your journey. And unless an individual persists in the face of adversity, they will be doomed to fail.

Did you know that the average time for a person to become a millionaire is 22 years?[108]

Think about that for a moment.

So if you are not at your goal when you want to be, just keep on going.

When you start on your quest for liquid riches, it often feels pretty tough–but it does get easier once you have built up momentum. For six days a week, and sometimes seven, I train on a Life Fitness™ cross training machine. The first 20 minutes of my hour period is always the hardest. But once I am through that first 20 minutes, my breathing is more controlled, my legs don't ache as much and I feel much more positive about achieving my end goal.

This is very much like building wealth. It might seem a little awkward at first but once you have built up that momentum, like a plane that has just taken off, you are able to ease gently back on the throttle into what will be a very enjoyable flight. Some people ask why I cross train as much as I do. And when they do, I always share with them what I believe to be the enormous benefits. And these benefits help your health *and* your wealth.

And if you think about it, your overall health and wellbeing will always play a major role in building wealth. Put simply, a person who is strong and healthy in mind and body is going to respond much better to adversity compared with a person who is unhealthy. And I am sure that you will agree that a person who is unhealthy is therefore the more likely of the two to give up when the going gets tough.

Another example of why I train as often as I do, comes from William Glasser's outstanding book; *Positive Addiction*. Glasser states that vigorous daily exercising (such as running or cross training) helps you to build mental strength which in turn helps you to persist–which then helps you to stay the course until goal completion. I remember Glasser saying something that made a huge impact on me. He said, most people know *what* to do and even *how* to do it, but they do not have the *mental strength* to follow through. And if you are ambitious like me and you agree with Glasser's message, you might decide to do whatever you can–from this point onwards–to improve and increase your mental strength.

How to Live Your Dream Lifestyle Now

We are now closing in on the finish line and before we start to wrap things up, there is something very important that I want to share with you. In Chapter 2, you learned about how having enough cash can help you to create your dream lifestyle. The thing is, there is no reason why you can't start creating it right now. Once you are clear on what would be the ideal for you, you can immediately start to make choices and decisions that will result in turning your thoughts and pictures into your dream reality.

To put it another way, you have the power to start making your dream lifestyle a reality…right now. Yes of course, parts of your dream lifestyle may need more money than you have at this moment in time, but there is nothing stopping you from starting the process. This is something that Paul and I have been doing since we began our Financial Freedom journey back in the late nineties.

We started making the changes to our own lives when we had very little in savings and investments. All we did was think a bit smarter and make more intelligent decisions. And it is really simple how to go about it. All you do is start to piece together your dream lifestyle, bit by bit. For example, if your dream lifestyle involves eating at Michelin star restaurants on a weekly basis, then what is stopping you from eating at Michelin star restaurants right now?

Granted, to eat there every week may stretch your current budget, but nothing's stopping you from eating there every once in a while. In other words, you could eat at a Michelin star restaurant once a year as a treat, every quarter, or even once a month if you could afford it and it didn't bite into your long-term savings and investment plan.

This type of thinking can be applied to every part of your dream lifestyle. And when you get it right, each year, as you move closer and closer towards your end goal, your lifestyle will adapt and become more and more like the ideal lifestyle that you want so badly.

I also suggest that you think hard about what you currently do with your time on a daily, weekly and monthly basis. Try to identify what things you are doing that are causing you stress, unhappiness or anxiety. What are the things that you are doing that make you feel out of control?

Whatever your answer is, these are the things that you want to be stopping doing–or not doing as much of.

On the flip side, also identify things that make you feel good. The things you highlight are the things that you want to be doing more of.

You see, when it comes to time and tasks, you can do only one of four things. You can do *more* of something, you can do *less* of something, you can *stop* doing something and finally you can *start* to do something.

By focusing on what you want to do more of, what you want to do less of, what you feel you would like to start doing and what you know you need to stop, your life will transform dramatically.

It is a very simple idea but with remarkable consequences.

Paul and I made the conscious decision a long time ago that we were going to stop putting ourselves in situations that caused us unease and start spending more time on things that gave us pleasure–and made us feel happy. By taking time to really think about what we were both doing with our lives, we recognised people, situations and circumstances that were causing us pain and then made a decision to phase them out.

We also recognised the things that we loved to do, and people that we felt great about spending time with. And all we did was start to spend more time on these things we enjoyed and made a more conscious effort to see the people we connected with much more often.

Some of the things we identified that caused us discomfort we stopped immediately.

And by doing this, the relief we felt–when we realised that we were in control of our lives and we did not have to do anything that we didn't want–was and is extremely liberating.

If for any reason you think that this will not work for you, I suggest that you give it a try just to see if it makes any difference to how you feel about your life in general. You never know, it could make a big difference. Plus you have nothing to lose and so much to gain.

How to Maximize Your Probability of Success

Before we say our goodbyes, I would like to point out that in our world there are many doom-mongers. These people, who seem to see the glass always half empty, are always going to find a reason not to believe the ideas, strategies and overall philosophy that we have covered throughout this book. When you are excited about what you have learned and you try to share it with them, they may not be as enthusiastic as you are. This could include your partner, your family, your friends or your work colleagues.

When you talk to them about things such as making superior tax-free returns using ISA Trend Investing, they may scoff and sneer and try to put your new ideas down. Please do not be discouraged by what they say. Instead, keep your thoughts to yourself and do not try to convince them because they have probably already made up their minds that it does not work. Why waste your time and effort when it can be put to much better use?

Let them laugh, let them ridicule and let them try to embarrass you because you will know that one glorious day, if you stick with this system and follow the rules, you will retire liquid rich.

And where will they be?

Businessman, philanthropist and bestselling author W. Clement Stone once wrote, *"Whatever the mind of man can conceive and believe, it can achieve."*

Belief that you *can* and *will* make it is vital to your success.

My friend, it is now time for me to sign off, but before I go let me say these final words. I like to think of myself as a positive realist. I simply cannot prove my predictions, but what I can say is that past, proven results plus logic suggests that the things I predict will probably happen.

Winston Churchill was once asked to give some advice to a business school on how to be successful and he stood up and said, *"Never, never, never, never, never, never, never, never, never give up,"* and then he proceeded to sit back in his chair. With Winston's words of wisdom, I bid you farewell and look forward to possibly meeting you in the near future. I am already excited about hearing your amazing story of how you conquered adversity, broke through and ended up realising your wildest financial dreams.

Notes

1. Nasdaq: At the time of the writing, Nasdaq trading at 2438.49
    - 7th May 2008.

2. www.statistics.gov.uk

    PDF document - Name: First release - Internet Access 2007
    - Households and Individuals - 28th August 2007.

    http://www.statistics.gov.uk/pdfdir/inta0807.pdf

3. Michael Dell speaking in New Dehli, India, March 20, 2007.

    http://www.dell.com/content/topics/global.aspx/corp/pressoffice/
    en/2007/2007_03_20_ndi_000?c=us&1=en&s=corp

4. www.guardian.co.uk June 14th 2007.

    Article titled: Broadband Spreads the Globe - Written by
    Richard Wray, Communications Editor.

    Article states: "Almost 300 million people worldwide are now
    accessing the internet using fast broadband connections."

    http://www.guardian.co.uk/business/2007/jun/13/newmedia.
    media

5. www.research.att.com and www.Geek.com

    at & t labs research - www.research.att.com: Handbook of
    Optimization In Telecommunications.

In the period 1995 to 2001, the number of mobile phones worldwide grew from about 91 million to almost a billion.

www.Geek.com: According to specialist information provider Informa, there are now enough mobile phone subscriptions for half the world's population. More than 3.3 billion subscriptions now exist, and it has taken just 26 years to reach that figure.

http://www.geek.com/33-billion-mobile-phone-subscriptions-worldwide/ and http://www.research.att.com/~mgcr/hot.html

6. The author learned from the in-depth studies conducted by William O'Neil over a 50 year period–3 out of every 4 stocks moved in the same direction as the market. Because investment funds hold stocks, it was logical to the author that three out of every four funds would also move in the same direction as the market.

7. Morningstar.co.uk - The AXA Framlington Japan Fund.

8. Stephen Sutherland's personal ISA account annual returns vs the Nasdaq Composite annual returns.

9. Legg Mason - Period taken 25th October 2005 (NAV price 268.5) to 16th January 2006 (NAV price 402).

10. Morningstar.co.uk - 5 year performance results taken Feb 5th 2008.

11. Morningstar.co.uk

    Invesco Perpetual Latin America Fund performance Dec 31st 2002 to December 31st 2007.

12. Morningstar.co.uk

    Scottish Widows Latin America Fund performance Dec 31st 2002 to December 31st 2007.

13.　　How to Make Money In Stocks: A Winning System in Good Times or Bad, 3rd Edition - William J. O'Neil.

Page 18 "...History demonstrates that most bull (up) markets tend to last two to four years and are followed by a recession or bear (down) market; then another bull market starts..."

Investors.com - Ask IBD - Question: What does the term 'secular bear market' mean?

Answer: A secular bear market is one that is not seasonal or cyclical in nature. It is a bear market that lasts longer than the nine to 18 months that typical bear markets last.

http://investdaily.custhelp.com/cgi-bin/investdaily.cfg/php/enduser/std_adp.php?p_faqid=91&p_created=1003302000&p_sid=PbqOHn3j&p_accessibility=0&p_redirect=&p_lva=&p_sp=cF9zcmNoPTEmcF9zb3J0X2J5PSZwX2dyaWRzb3J0PSZwX3Jvd19bnQ9MzgsMzgmcF9wcm9kcz0mcF9jYXRzPTEwJnBfcHY9JnBfY3Y9MS4xMCZwX3BhZ2U9MSZwX3N1YXJjaF90ZXh0PSI5IHRvIDE4IG1vbnRocyI*&p_li=&p_topview=1

14.　　Nasdaq Period 31st October 2007 to 17th March 2008.

15.　　ISACO's stance on the market changed from Unhealthy to Healthy on the 25th April 2008.

16.　　Author's overall return (including capital additions) on his ISA account from 1997 to year ending 2007.

17.　　May 2008.

18.　　Nasdaq: (March 10th 1980 - March 10th 2000).

19.　　Nasdaq: (March 10th 1975 - March 10th 2000).

20. Nationwide Building Society - House prices had seen little or no price changes over the previous 10 year period.

21. UK Land Registry (Average house price in England & Wales 1995: £67,685 & 2006: £213,179).

22. Nasdaq (10th March 1998 - 10th March 2008).

23. Answers.com.

    http://www.answers.com/topic/trend?cat=biz-fin

24. InvestorDictionary.com.

    http://www.investordictionary.com/definition/trend+trading.aspx

25. The author's personal opinion.

26. Yahoo Finance - Period taken 29th Dec 89 to 31st Dec 1999.

27. ISACO: ISACO's Tax-Free Millionaire various multi year packages allow the client to shadow invest what the owners of the business are doing with their tax-free money.

28. Stephen and Paul Sutherland joint Ameritrade account: Period 1st May 2000 - (Ameritrade account value $31,409) to 10th July 2003 (Ameritrade account value $1,284,826.94).

29. 24 Essential Lessons for Investment Success: Learn the Most Important Investment Techniques from the Founder of Investor's Business Daily - William J. O'Neil.

    Page 81 "...I have never missed the very beginning of a new bull market with this method of tracking the general market indices carefully."

    Note: The author follows William O'Neil's philosophy of reading, analysing and timing the market.

30.   The author attended Anthony Robbins's Wealth Mastery in Oct 1999.

31.   The speaker in question at Wealth Mastery was Mr Chris Manning.

32.   The author considered O'Neil a "leading authority" due to O'Neil's impressive achievements such as:

1. 40% annualised returns over a 10 year period (source Market Wizards - Jack Schwager).

2. A 20-fold increase in his account in 26 months.

3. Not missing the start of every bull market in the last 50 years.

4. Being a bestselling author - How to Make Money in Stocks was the biggest selling investment book in 1988.

5. In 1984, launching a financial newspaper (Investors Business Daily) that was and still is a direct competitor to the highly acclaimed Wall Street Journal.

6. O'Neil's experience in the stock market since 1958.

7. Advising the big institutional clients on what stocks to buy and sell.

8. After conducting a 50 year study on "how the market works" O'Neil pioneered and developed the use of historical precedent to analyze equities in tandem with fundamental and technical analysis. Drawing from these discoveries, he created the CAN SLIM® - A proven tested way of making money in the stock market.

9. Due to O'Neil's success, he purchased a seat on the New York Stock Exchange at the young age of 30.

Note: Most of O'Neil's achievements can be found at <u>www. williamoneil.com</u> by going to his biography.

<u>http://www.williamoneil.com/About/WilliamJONeil.aspx</u>

33.   24 Essential Lessons for Investment Success: Learn the Most Important Investment Techniques from the Founder of Investor's Business Daily - William J. O'Neil.

Page 81… "I have never missed the very beginning of a new bull market with this method of tracking the general market indices carefully."

34.   <u>www.WilliamONeil.com</u>

William J. O'Neil Biography.

"….He quickly became the top performing broker in his firm. After a 20-fold increase in his own account in 26 months, Mr. O'Neil branched out on his own and founded William O'Neil + Co. Incorporated in 1963."

<u>http://www.williamoneil.com/About/WilliamJONeil.aspx</u>

35.   <u>DailyGraphs.com</u>.

Complete Equity Research package consists of Daily Graphs Online® Daily Graphs® Custom Screen Wizard and Daily Graphs® Industry Groups.

36.   The author attended the Investors Business Daily's one day Advanced Investors Workshops twice. The first he attended was held in a hotel in South Beach, Miami in 2001 and the second in a hotel in New York 2002.

37.   Stephen's 2000 performance 1.31% gain vs Nasdaq's 39.29% loss.

38. In 2001 the Nasdaq Composite dropped 21.05% vs the author's gain of 31.74%.

39. Citywire.

40. How to Make Money In Stocks: A Winning System in Good Times or Bad, 3rd Edition - William J. O'Neil - Page 68.

41. Even though the market bottomed in Oct 2002, the bull market was not made official until March 17th 2003.

42. Yahoo Finance - Performance result taken October 9th 2001 SINA made a low of $1.02 - 27th Jan 2004 SINA made a high of $49.50.

43. Yahoo Finance - Performance result taken April 9th 2001 SOHU made a low of $0.52 -15th July 2003 SOHU made a high of $43.40.

44. Daily Graphs - Performance result taken July 2001 NTES made a low of $0.13 - Oct 2003 NTES made a high of $18.00 (March 2006 4/1 stock split adjusted price).

45. With additional funds added to the author's joint trading account of $416,472.90, the author's trading account has a total capital starting point of $523,165.76. With the account being valued at $1,284,826.94 on Thursday 10th July, the amount gained was $761,661 (a 145.6% 7 month gain).

46. The author and his brother were financially independent when scored against the following definition of financial independence.

Financial Independence: To have accumulated an amount of money so large that you are no longer influenced or controlled by others to sustain a *comfortable* lifestyle.

47. The New Psycho-Cybernetics - Maxwell Maltz and edited and updated by Dan S. Kennedy - Page 15.

48. The New Psycho-Cybernetics - Maxwell Maltz and edited and updated by Dan S. Kennedy - Page 29.

49. The New Psycho-Cybernetics - Maxwell Maltz and edited and updated by Dan S. Kennedy - Page 42.

50. Success Secrets of Self-Made Millionaires - Brian Tracy.

51. Brian Tracy's Maximum Achievement.

52. ISACO's Tax-Free Millionaire ISA Shadow Investing System.

53. HIRE CAR™ - A 7 step investment fund research tool.

54. ISACO's Tax-Free Millionaire ISA Shadow Investing System.

55. Nasdaq.

56. Morningstar.co.uk.

57. Nasdaq.

58. The author noticed (when researching the market back to 1893), the indexes have always eventually made new highs.

59. UK Land Registry (average house price on England & Wales 1995: £67,685 & 2006: £213,179).

60. Yahoo Finance - S&P 500 - On 31st Dec 1969, the S&P 500 closed at 91.25 - On Dec 31st 1979, the S&P 500 closed at 107.94

    Price progress made over 10 year period was +18.3% or +1.7% annualised.

61. Yahoo Finance: +18.3% average annual return over period March 10th 1975 - March 10th 2000.

62. Based on financial description of a typical ISACO premium client (see below).

Case Study 1

Married 35 Years old.

High Income.

Tax-Free Savings: No

Case Study 2

Married 45 Years old.

High Income.

Tax-Free Savings: £250,000

Case Study 3

Married 50 Years old.

High Income.

Tax-Free Savings: £650,000

63. High income equates to approximately £70,000 net or more per annum.

64. This is based on the stock market putting in a very strong performance—such as the performance from 1990-2000 plus the investor having a high degree of knowledge in how things such as the stock market, investment funds, timing the market, ISAs and SIPPs work.

65. ManUTDZone.com.

As of May 11th 2008, Sir Alex Ferguson is the most successful manager in British football history with 14 major trophies in England, not to mention the trophies he won at Aberdeen. He has won five FA Cup Finals - no other manager has achieved this in England.

Ferguson has been premier league manager of the year 7 times: 1994, 1996, 1997, 1999, 2000 and 2003. He has won the manager of the month award 19 times. For years the accusation had been levelled that Ferguson had only won the European Cup once so could therefore not be considered a true great. By winning against Chelsea in Moscow in 2008, Ferguson had shut his critics up once and for all. A second champions' league put him well above his peers.

http://www.manutdzone.com/playerpages/SirAlexFerguson. htm

66. It is possible to check past investment recommendations by looking at the investments performance and comparing it with one of the main stock indexes such as the FTSE 100 or the S&P 500 to see if the investment "outperformed" the market. This can be done by looking at past data on sites such as Morningstar. co.uk.

67. Financial Times October 8 / October 9 2005 weekend edition. Advert page 9 - Pick the brains of the best stock pickers - John Lee's bio mentions "His PEP and ISA portfolios are currently valued at over £1m from a base cost of £140,000."

68. Telegraph.co.uk.

Edition: 10th February 2007 - Your Money section article by Kara Gammell.

Sub-headline: Investing with PEP and ISA allowances, a Kent couple built up a £1m-plus fund in just 20 years.

Mentions in article "…and now hold a portfolio worth more than £1.3m."

http://www.telegraph.co.uk/money/main.jhtml?xml=/money/2007/02/10/cmtax10.xml

69. Barclays Stockbrokers - Barclays Stockbrokers ISAs seminar.

http://www.mediazone.brighttalk.com/comm/Barclays Stockbrokers/7e53459277-7011-314-6514

70. At the time of writing (11th May 2008) the Government had not imposed any limits that ISA portfolio values could grow into.

71. www.hm-treasury.gov.uk

Individual Savings Accounts (ISAs)

ISAs are available indefinitely;

All Personal Equity Plans (PEPs) will automatically become stocks and shares ISAs.

Savers can transfer money saved in cash ISAs into stocks and shares ISAs.

A new structure and limits, removing the Mini/Maxi distinction. From April 2008, every adult will have an annual ISA investment allowance of £7,200. Up to £3,600 of that allowance can be saved in cash with one provider. The remainder of the £7,200 allowance can be invested in stocks and shares with either the same or another provider.

http://www.hm-treasury.gov.uk/documents/financial_services/savings/topics_savings_isas.cfm

72.   William O'Neil's CAN SLIM™ System of investing.

73.   Investors.com/MediaCenter and TFNN.com - Tom O'Brien
      interviewing William O'Neil - March 11th 2008.

      http://www.investors.com/MediaCenter/?MediaID=993&t=A
      (Subscription to Investors Business Daily required to view).

74.   Investors.com/MediaCenter and www.TFNN.com - Tom
      O'Brien interviewing William O'Neil - March 11th 2008.

      http://wwwinvestors.com/MediaCenter/?MediaID=993&t=A
      (Subscription to Investors Business Daily required to view).

75.   The Tax-Free Millionaire System of Investing forced the author,
      his brother, his team and his clients out of the market into
      the safety of a cash based fund on the 28th February 2007.
      They then remained out of the market until April 25th 2008,
      completely avoiding the up and coming bear market (Nasdaq
      24.7% correction Oct 31st to March 17th) that started in the last
      quarter of 2007 - Note: Bear markets are normally defined by
      many market watchers as a correction on a main index of 20%
      or more.

76.   Performance taken Thursday January 24th 2008 - Nasdaq fell
      19% in previous 3 month period versus Fidelity MoneyBuilder
      Income Fund (Cash based fund) +2% in previous 3 month
      period.

77.   It is based on William O'Neil's investment results, IBD reader's
      results, author's results plus author's clients' results. It's also
      based on the Tax-Free Millionaire Investment system beating
      the Nasdaq Composites performance. And finally, it's based on
      author's ISA account returns versus the Nasdaq Composite.
      Period taken was Dec 31st 2003 to Jan 5th 2008.

78.   It is based on author's estimation on how accurate the ISACO
      timing system is.

79.   At the beginning of 2008, 1 year Tax-Free Millionaire ISA Shadow Investing packages were being sold at £2995.

80.   The Successful Investor: What 80 Million People Need to Know to Invest Profitably and Avoid Big Losses - William J. O'Neil.

Page 22 "Institutional or Professional Investors - many of whom manage portfolios in the tens of billions of dollars - account for about 75 percent of all important market activity (if you omit program trading)."

81.   Period taken was Dec 31st 2003 to Jan 5th 2008.

82.   Author's return on his ISA account for 2004 without any capital additions added.

83.   Date results taken 18th of Jan 2008 - The Nasdaq was down 11.5% and the Tax-Free Millionaire system was up 0.6%.

84.   Period taken was Dec 31st 2003 to Jan 5th 2008.

85.   Yahoo Finance - 23rd Dec 1974 to March 10th 2000.

86.   Author's best estimation on how many funds, when screened, actually pass the HIRE CAR™ criteria.

87.   2 year performance return on author's SIPP account (without any capital additions).

88.   The author's own personal estimation.

89.   ISACO 283 premium clients - February 2008.

90.   In the past, the author and his brother Paul taught the Tax-Free Millionaire System of Investing at a live 4 hour event. After the events, feedback forms were distributed and clients were asked if they would recommend the system to others. In October 2007, 91% of attendees said they would recommend to others.

91.   Author's personal estimation.

92.   How to Make Money in Stocks - William J. O'Neil Third edition - Page 49.

93.   Author's return on his ISA account for 2004 without any capital additions added.

94.   Author's personal estimation. Note: Based on the author's 10 year experience - plus backed with the knowledge that according to William O'Neil in How to Make Money in Stocks - Third Edition - page 40 "...the most desirable growth stocks tend to correct 1 to 2 times the general market."

      This point is relevant due to the funds HIRE CAR™ finds, generally hold the market's most desirable growth stocks.

95.   Brian Tracy's Change Your Thinking, Change Your Life: How to Unlock Your Full Potential for Success and Achievement - Page 47.

96.   www.CDC.gov

      http://www.cdc.gov/nchs/data/nvsr53_06t12.pdf

97.   www.actuaries.org.uk

      http://www.actuaries.org.uk/_data/assets/pdf_file/0019/1933/ pensionscom_secondreportpaper1_resp.pdf

98.   www.CDC.gov

      http://www.cdc.gov/nchs/data/dvs/nvsr53_06t12.pdf

99.   www.CDC.gov

      http://www.cdc.gov/nchs/data/dvs/nvsr53_06t12.pdf

100. The Psychology of Winning - Dr Denis Waitley.

    1. Young Aborigine - page 80.

    2. Fortune teller - voodoo death - page 80.

    3. Woman having operation - pages 80/81.

    4. Elvis - page 81.

101. Maxwell Malz's The New Psycho-Cybernetics. Pages 73 and 74.

102. Can be found in Appendix B - Recommended Reading / Audio.

103. E*Trade is one such company with low trading charges. Note: Author does not endorse E*Trade.

104. Prices as of May 2008.

105. William O'Neil's How to Make Money in Stocks Workshop Series - Levels I, II, and III.

106. William O'Neil's How to Make Money in Stocks Workshop Series - Level IV CAN SLIM™ Masters Program.

107. Daily Express - Saturday January 7th 2006 Edition.

108. Brian Tracy's Success Mastery Academy audio program.

APPENDIX A

Words of Praise from Delighted Clients

John Bristow, a businessman living in Newport, had an ISA account portfolio of £21,515 before learning the Tax-Free Millionaire system. So far **he has managed to grow his portfolio by 243%.** He recently told us that his account is valued at over £74,000. His words were, "*I have complete confidence in the system.*"

Sarah Readings, an executive coach and coach trainer from Leeds, **had zero in tax-free savings** before discovering this brand new way to invest. **In just 16 months, her account grew into £29,166–and recently it was valued at £56,280.** When asked about how things were going, her answer was, "*I do believe that the system will be very successful in the long-term and I believe that I can reach my target of Financial Freedom in the next 10-15 years.*"

Jon Marshall, a partnership development manager from Cheshire, was another individual **who had zero in tax-free savings** before learning the secrets of the 3 minutes per day shadow investing system. So far **he has managed to build up an account valued at over £46,000.** He was thrilled when he made 21% within a 3 month period. Jon has seen the power of the system at work on profiting from the big upside moves and also the protection it gives you on the downside.

When Stephen recently spoke to Jon, he was ecstatic about being in cash when the 2007 bear market struck and the Nasdaq fell a horrible 24.7%. His words were, "*It's a good job the system told us to get out onto the sidelines. If we hadn't got out of the market, I would have lost a lot of money.*

Shadow investing has saved me a packet. If we had been invested during that downturn, my portfolio would have been bleeding substantial losses."

Glenn Warhurst is another fan of the system. Glenn, a business owner and property investor said, *"I recently achieved an amazing milestone with my ISA investment. In just 16 months I made a 50% increase. I have also achieved a great return on my SIPP pension of approximately 16% in a little over 11 months. Gaynor, my wife, is also up about 33% after just 13 months. I have 100% faith in the system."*

Joe De Beer, a mechanical engineer from Finchley Central, London, recently said, *"The system works! In just 15 weeks I've made an amazing 16.1% gain on my portfolio. And this is only the beginning!"*

Eric Taylor, a retired accountant, had this to say, *"I have been busy organising my ISAs, and trading on the stock market. Overall, the funds have increased by 15.3%."*

Another excited client, Andrew Bute from Kent said, *"I subscribed to the Daily Market Updates about 6 weeks ago and made my first investment shortly after. So far I have seen growth of 10.4% -all looks pretty good so far."*

Michael Garland, a private investor who lives in West Yorkshire, started using the shadow investing system with quite a substantial amount in tax-free savings that he'd previously built up. Michael saw almost immediate gains on his portfolio, and said, *"I just love the Tax-Free Millionaire '3 Minutes per Day' system—it really does work. In just two and a half months, my wife and I have made a 767% return on the money it cost us to pay for the package. Wow, what a great investment!"*

Stephen and his brother Paul managed to get their parents into the system. Even after their dad was gifted his Bentley, he was still sceptical, due to having a negative association with the stock market. However, he is not sceptical any more. He made 48.1% in his first year of following the system.

Here are some further comments from delighted Clients:

David Redbond - Chief Information Officer of a FTSE 250 Financial Company - Gloucestershire, UK.

"10 / 10 for valuable content."

"Definitely recommend."

Bob Sweeney - Pioneer of Health Clubs in the UK & Professional Investor - Halifax, UK.

"I was truly convinced."

"Wow factor 9 / 10."

"Definitely recommend."

David Vernon - Hedge Fund Manager - London, UK.

"HIRE CAR, the secret investing formula is outstanding."

"9 / 10."

"Strongly recommend."

Stephen Swinbank - Professional Investor & Chair of Trustees, NCR Ltd Pension Fund - Bedfordshire, UK.

"I liked meeting the Sutherland brothers and their collegues, very professional yet humble and genuine people who take a real interest in their clients. Thank you. I would recommend this to others."

"Credibility, integrity and the support team - 10 / 10."

Nirpal Bharaj - Treasurer at Kodak - Ilford, UK.

"ISACO's secret investing formula was excellent."

"Definitely Recommend."

"10 / 10."

Chris Davies - Property Investor - Sheffield - UK.

"Very valuable and very exciting information."

"The concept is LIFE CHANGING."

Alan Jones – Business Owner – Windsor, UK.

"What I like most is that there is no hype—it's all solid information."

"Strongly recommend."

Nick Sinfield - Physiotherapist - St Albans, UK.

"I loved the simplicity of the Tax-Free Millionaire System, with easy to follow and exciting information. Outstanding."

"HIRE CAR™, the secret investing formula that helps you to find the "best of the best funds" is outstanding."

"Strongly recommend."

Branwen Edwards - Retired - Sunbury-on-Thames, UK.

"What I liked most was that there was lots of support if needed, and the fact that HIRE CAR™ only takes just 3 minutes per day is outstanding."

"Integrity - 10 / 10."

"Strongly recommend."

John Tanqueray - G.P. And Company Director - Northampton, UK.

"Clear, well structured and made me feel comfortable. The overall system is outstanding."

"Credibility and integrity - 10 / 10."

" Strongly recommend."

Richard Benn - Business Analyst - Manchester, UK.

"Very clear presentation of information, and your secret investing formula (HIRE CAR™) blew me away."

"Credibility and integrity - 10 / 10."

Veryan Farr - Property Investor - Dunblane, UK.

"The Tax-Free Millionaire System is easy to understand and quite simply outstanding!"

"Valuable content - 10 / 10."

"Strongly recommend."

Matthew Hale - Business Performance Manager - Sheffield, UK.

"Very good answers given to all the questions, clear and concise. Very informative, High level of detail and generated great interest.   Outstanding."

"Credibility - 10 / 10."

"Strongly recommend."

Joanne Addington - Head of Human Resources - Huntingdon, UK.

"I have great confidence in the system, and the support team has made me feel like a VIP—outstanding!"

"The Tax-Free Millionaire System overall just knocked me over."

"Credibility and integrity - 10 / 10."

Gwyn Martyn - Business Owner - St Albans, UK.

"I think that HIRE CAR™ and your Tax-Free Millionaire System are outstanding!"

"Strongly recommend."

Adam Cox - Company Director - London, UK.

"Valuable information, and communicated very well. A very good use of my time. Thanks to the whole team. Outstanding!"

"Valuable content - 10 / 10."

"Strongly recommend."

Richard Parker - Partner - Wrexham, UK.

"Valuable content and credibility and expertise in subject matters -9 / 10."

Achel Mishra - Doctor - Newcastle-Upon-Tyne, UK.

"OUTSTANDING!"

"Clean communication, jargon free and empowering - 10 / 10."

John Mitchell - Professional Property Investor - Newport Pagnell, UK.

"I have total belief in the system."

"Definitely recommend."

David Freer - Business Owner - Royton, UK.

"Very professional."

"Now I believe it is possible to earn returns via the stock market of 20-30%."

"Credibility - 10 / 10."

Simon Patmore - Solicitor - Whitley Bay, UK.

"I am a true believer in your system."

"Credibility - 9 /10 "

Jag Patel - Professional Stock Market Investor - Leicester, UK.

"10 / 10 for valuable content."

Christopher Sturdy - Property Developer - Kent, UK.

"I liked the Sutherland brothers' psychology of investing."

"Straightforwardly explained and easy to follow with all the help one could need."

"A genuine enthusiasm for their subject and professional interest in their clients."

Terry Jacques - Professional Investor - Macclesfield, UK.

"Belief is crucial to success!"

"Credibility - 9 / 10."

"Definitely recommend."

Louis Hirshorn - Business Owner - Hampshire, UK.

"Lots of information in a short space of time–to the point!"

"9 /10 for credibility and the support team."

"Good sound investment strategy - Definitely recommend."

Steven Jackson - Property Investor /Developer - Scunthorpe, UK.

"All simple, believable and achievable."

"Definitely recommend - 9 / 10."

Maurice Beverley - Professional Investor - Oldham, UK.

"Integrity - 10 / 10."

"Definitely recommend."

Helen Palmer - Luxury Travel Broker - Barcelona, Spain.

"Credibility - 10 / 10."

"Definitely recommend."

Tony Ferraro - Partner - Northampton, UK.

"Stephen and Paul seem like straightforward, honest guys who want to help. It gave me a warm feeling. "

"Credibility - 10 / 10."

Paul Faghy - Account Manager - Durham, UK.

"I liked having the opportunity to share in the knowledge and experience of individuals' expertise that has taken them years to accumulate. Excellent!"

"Credibility - 10 / 10."

"Strongly recommend."

William Laundon - Professional Property Investor - Dorset, UK.

"9 / 10 - I virtually never give a 10."

"It was really excellent."

Nisha Desai - Pharmacist - Bromley, UK.

"I think the Tax-Free Millionaire 3 Minutes Per Day System is excellent."

"Credibility - 9 / 10 "

"Strongly Recommend."

Richard Turner - Property Investor - Bristol, UK.

"What I liked most was the simplicity of the system - 9.5 / 10."

Ben Ticehurst - Interim Manager - Oxford, UK.

"What I liked most was the integrity and NO SPIN."

"It delivered more than expected and was full of valuable content. I would definitely recommend - 9/10."

John Aigbokhaode - IT Contractor - Borehamwood, UK.

"The information is priceless—I am excited about the future."

"Definitely recommend."

Bill Tregellas - Property Letting - Barnstable, UK.

"People do not realise the importance of tax-free ISA's."

"Credibility - 10 /10."

"Definitely recommend."

Rizwan Kayani - Consultant - Nottinghamshire, UK.

"Outstanding - 10 / 10."

Trevor Sims - E-Bay Business Entrepreneur - Staffordshire, UK.

"Easy to understand - Definitely recommend - 10 / 10."

David Morris - Surveyor - Aberdeen, UK.

"Value for money - Definitely recommend - 9 / 10."

Rob Sheil - IT Consultant - Northamptonshire, UK.

"Very, very good!!–Questions answered fully."

Denis Brooks - Business Owner - Glazebury, UK.

"I wouldn't have changed a thing."

"Definitely recommend."

Des Ironside - Regional Manager - Wiltshire, UK.

"There aren't many opportunities like this."

"Definitely recommend."

Nigel Coward - Commercial Director - Dorchester, UK.

"Very informative, would definitely recommend - 9 / 10."

Nigel Fletcher - Sales Manager - Chelmarsh, UK.

"Strategy explained in an easy and understandable way—I think your determination to help others is fantastic—would recommend."

Alan Miller - Entrepreneur - Maidenhead, UK.

"Outstanding - 10 / 10."

Neil McCrimmon - Enviromental Health Officer - Walington, UK.

"10 / 10 for credibility."

Nigel Dell - Business Owner - Plymouth, UK.

"I liked the clarity of the information, it was easy to understand. Would recommend."

Dick Fisher - Entrepreneur - Stafford, UK.

"Detailed approach and answered all questions."

"WOW factor 9 / 10."

Paul Moone - Commercial Analyst - St Albans, UK.

"I loved the simple breakdown of principles and idea's behind the system, and the fact that it takes just 3 minutes a day--WOW!"

"You have met all my expectations and have left me feeling very excited and motivated."

"Credibility - 10 / 10."

Mark Phillips - Senior Process Engineer - Loughborough, UK.

"The Tax-Free Millionaire System is outstanding, and all my questions were answered thoroughly. I have great confidence to get started."

"Credibility - 10 / 10."

"Strongly recommend."

Andrew Haney - Project Manager - Loughton, UK.

"The support team does an outstanding job of making me feel like a VIP!"

"Easy to understand, and I like the high level of information."

"Overall - 10 / 10."

"Strongly recommend."

David Waring - Museum Collections Officer - West Bromwich, UK.

"Wow, HIRE CAR™, the secret investing formula that takes only 3 Minutes Per Day is amazing!"

"Credibility and Wow factor - 10 / 10."

"Strongly recommend."

Matt Swarbrick - Writer - London, UK and Moscow, Russia.

"Clear explanations and details, keeps everything simple, and the secret investing formula (HIRE CAR™) is great!"

Saddat Abid - Project Manager - West Yorkshire, UK.

"Wow! The support service that you offer for HIRE CAR™, where it takes just 3 Minutes per Day, and the secret investing formula that picks the very best investment funds is incredible!"

"Overall - 10 / 10."

"Strongly Recommend."

Rachel Grant - Strategic Alliance Manager - London, UK.

"Truly a great system."

"Outstanding integrity - 10 / 10."

"Definitely recommend—I have total belief."

Raghbir Aujla - IT Engineer - Essex, UK.

"Simple, easy to understand, and with great support afterwards."

"Definitely recommend."

APPENDIX B

Recommended Reading /Audio

In this next section, you will discover a list of recommended books and audio programs. Prior to 1998, I could have listed the number of books that I'd read on one hand, but as you will see, over the last ten years, I've been pretty busy.

Most of my recommendations are what are known as "how to" books and "how to" audio programs.

I just think it's amazing that you can plug into the greatest minds that have ever lived—and learn their best "how to" tips, strategies and techniques.

Reading books and listening to audio programs means you can spend time with an expert (the author) who will share with you all their juiciest secrets of success and for very little cost. My thinking is, why try to re-invent the wheel when you can follow in the footsteps of already successful people?

When you look at my recommendations, you'll notice I have split the books and audio programs into different categories. You may be surprised or curious to know why I have included books and audio on subjects that are not money or investment related. There are some very good reasons.

Let me explain.

One reason is connected to my personal philosophy on how to live a good life. My philosophy is based on four key elements; to learn, to serve, to love and to experience. In other words, we all know that money is important, but we all know that our health and relationships are of much greater importance.

This is why you'll find recommendations under headings such as "Personal Development", "Health" and "Spiritual." And so if you are like me and agree that there is more to life than just money, you might like some of my choices that do not fall under the headings "Investing" and "Personal Finance."

I decided to recommend books and audio programs connected to business, sales and marketing because many of my clients are business owners. I think you'll agree that creating a successful business around something you are intensely passionate about is a great way to spend your time and slowly build your wealth.

Out of all the subject headings, I do strongly recommend that you consider learning sales and marketing. And that goes for whatever line of work you are involved in. The reason for this is tied to increasing your value, which I mention in more detail in Chapter 9. The rule is, if you want to be paid more, not only will you have to learn new skills and gain valuable knowledge, you'll also have to be able to sell and promote yourself so that others realise your true value.

You see, if we don't learn how to sell ourselves, we could end up being very frustrated by the progress we are making towards our financial goals. Having valuable knowledge or skills is no good unless a person can "sell" the reasons why they are worth the amount they are charging.

And with all this in mind, what I can promise you is this. The more you read and apply, the more you'll earn and the greater the amount you can save and invest each and every year. And the more you read and listen to educational audio programs, the faster you'll get to your goal—and you'll feel great—because deep down you'll know that day by day you'll be moving one step closer towards your intended target.

I just hope that you catch the same learning bug that Paul and I caught. Since we caught it, life has never been the same. In case you are wondering, the audio programs can be purchased through Nightingale Conant (Nightingale.com).

Happy learning!

Your friend,

Stephen.

Recommended Reading

Big Time Money Makers

Business @ The Speed of Thought - Bill Gates.
Losing My Virginity - Richard Branson.
The Way to the Top - Donald J. Trump.
How to Get Rich - Donald J. Trump.
Think Like a Billionaire - Donald J. Trump.
Grinding It out - Ray Kroc.
Direct from Dell - Michael Dell.
Made in America - Sam Walton.
Pour Your Heart Into It - Howard Schultz.
Screw It, Let's Do It! - Richard Branson.
Oprah Winfrey Speaks - Janet Lowe.

Investing

(Note: The 12 books in bold below are recommended by the author for people who wish to follow the "DIY" route and have a desire to become a full-time stock market investor.)

How to Make Money in Stocks - William O'Neil 2nd and 3rd Editions.
24 Essential Lessons for Investment Success - William O'Neil.
The Successful Investor - William O'Neil.
How to Make Money Selling Stocks Short - William O'Neil.
My Own Story - Bernard Baruch.

The Battle for Investment Survival - Gerald Loeb.
How to Trade in Stocks - Jesse Livermore.
How I Made $2,000,000 in the Stock Market - Nicolas Darvas.
One Up On Wall Street - Peter Lynch.
Market Wizards - Jack Schwager.
The New Market Wizards - Jack Schwager.
Reminiscences of a Stock Operator - Edwin Lefevre.
Investors Business Daily and the Making of Millionaires - David Saito-Chung.
Lessons from the Greatest Stock Traders of all Time - John Boik.
Secrets for Profiting in Bull and Bear Markets - Stan Weinstein.
No Bull - Michael Steinhardt.
Winning on Wall Street - Martin Zwieig.
Money Masters of our Time - John Train.
Tools and Tactics for the Master Day Trader - Oliver Velez.
The Technical Analysis Course - Thomas Meyers.
Pit Bull - Martin Schwartz.
The New Investment Superstars - Lois Peltz.
Growth & Income – How to Build a Mutual Fund Money Machine - Dr R. Bryan Stoker.
Come Into My Trading Room - Dr Alexander Elder.
Trading with Crowd Psychology - Carl Gyllenram.
Trade Your Way to Financial Freedom - Van K. Tharp.
Common Sense on Mutual Funds - John C. Bogle.
Trader Vic - Victor Sperandeo.
Taming the Lion - Richard Farleigh.
Making Hard Cash in a Soft Real Estate Market - Wendy Patton and Justin Ryan.
Nanotech Fortunes - Darrell Brookstein.
Property Magic - Simon Zutshi.
The Next Big Investment Boom - Mark Shipman.
The Bull Hunter - Dan Denning.
The Way of the Turtle - Curtis Faith.
Big Money, Little Effort - Mark Shipman.
Trend Trading for a Living - Dr Thomas K. Carr.
Mastering Trading Stress - Ari Kiev.
The Naked Trader - Robbie Burns.

Trading for Dummies - Michael Griffis and Lita Epstein.
Trend Trading - Daryl Guppy.
The Neatest Little Guide to Stock Market Investing - Jason Kelly.

Money General

Sold! The Origins of Money and Trade - Runestone Press.
A History of Money - Glyn Davies.
The Natural History of the Rich - Richard Conniff.

Personal Finance

Think and Grow Rich - Napoleon Hill.
The Science of Getting Rich - Wallace D. Wattles.
7 Strategies for Wealth and Happiness - Jim Rohn.
Money for Life - Alvin Hall.
The Richest Man in Babylon - George S. Clason.
Rich Dad Poor Dad - Robert Kiyosaki.
Cash Flow Quadrant - Robert Kiyosaki.
Rich Dad's Guide to Investing - Robert Kiyosaki.
Retire Young, Retire Rich - Robert Kiyosaki.
Make Your Child a Millionaire - Alan Oscroft.
The One Minute Millionaire - Mark Victor Hansen & Robert Allen.
The Instant Millionaire - Mark Fisher.
How to Think Like a Millionaire - Mark Fisher.
The Ten Percent Solution - Marc Allen.
Free Lunch - David Smith.
The Millionaire Next Door - Thomas J. Stanley.
How to Become a Millionaire - Jim Slater.
Multiple Streams of Internet Income - Robert Allen.
Getting Loaded - Peter Bielagus.
Grow Rich with Peace of Mind - Napoleon Hill.
Conversations with Millionaires - Mike Litman and Jason Oman.
The Automatic Millionaire - David Bach.
The Wealthy Barber - David Chilton.
Think Like a Tycoon - Bill "Tycoon" Greene.
Who Took My Money? - Robert Kiyosaki.
Automatic Wealth - Michael Masterson.

Mentored by a Millionaire - Steve K. Scott.
Getting Rich Your Own Way - Brian Tracy.
The Art of Money Getting - P T. Barnum.
Cracking the Millionaire Code - Mark Victor Hansen and Robert Allen.
Rich Dad's Guide to Becoming Rich - Robert Kiyosaki.
Seven Years to Seven Figures - Michael Masterson.
How to Get Rich - Felix Dennis.
Napoleon Hill's A Year of Growing Rich - Napoleon Hill.
Your Money or Your Life - Joe Dominguez and Vicki Robin.
Don't Worry Make Money - Richard Carlson.
How to Think Like a Millionaire - Charles Albert Poissant with Christian Godefroy.

Business

The 100 Absolutely Unbreakable Laws of Business Success - Brian Tracy.
Customers.com - Patricia Seybold.
Principle Centred Leadership - Stephen Covey.
Shackleton's Way - Margot Morrell.
Work in Progress - Michael Eisner.
Dig Your Well Before You're Thirsty - Harvey Mackay.
Swim with the Sharks without Being Eaten Alive - Harvey Mackay.
The One Minute Manager - Ken Blanchard & Spencer Johnson.
Hire and Keep the Best People - Brian Tracy.
Harvard Business Review on Entrepreneurship - Harvard Business School Press.
The Five Temptations of a CEO - Patrick Lencioni.
Maximum Achievement - Brian Tracy.
Lincoln on Leadership - Donald T Phillips.
Iacocca – An Autobiography - Lee Iacocca.
Your Idea Can Make You Rich - Dragons Den - BBC.
The Beermat Entrepreneur - Mike Southon & Chris West.
Business as Unusual - Anita Roddick.
Ben and Jerrys Double Dip - Ben Cohen and Jerry Greenfield.
Winning - Jack Welch.
Good to Great - Jim Collins.
Instant CashFlow - Bradley J. Sugars.
E-Myth Mastery - Michael Gerber.

The E-Code - Joe Vitale and Jo Han Mok.

Built to Last - Jim Collins and Jerry Porras.

Growing a Business - Paul Hawkin.

Power and Persuasion - Michael Masterson.

Nuts! - Kevin & Jackie Freiberg.

No BS Time Management for Entrepreneurs - Dan Kennedy.

The 4-Hour Workweek - Timothy Ferriss.

What They Don't Teach You at Harvard Business School - Mark McCormack.

The Incredible Secret Money Machine - Don Lancaster.

Blue Ocean Strategy - W. Chan Kim and Renee Mauborgne.

Ready Fire Aim - Michael Masterson.

The Star Principle - Richard Koch.

The Effective Executive - Peter F. Drucker.

Choose and Grow Your Business in 90 Days - Wendy Evans.

The Global Technology Revolution - Richard Silberglitt.

Billionaire in Training - Bradley J. Sugars.

The Achievers Profile - Allan Cox.

The Discipline of Market Leaders - Michael Treacy & Fred Wiersema.

Sales and Marketing

Customers for Life - Carl Sewell.

Permission Marketing - Seth Godin.

Unleashing the Idea Virus - Seth Godin.

Raving Fans - Ken Blanchard.

The Nordstrom Way - Robert Spector.

How to Win Customers - Heinz Goldman.

Internet Marketing - Dave Chaffrey.

Customer Satisfaction Is Worthless - Jeffrey Gitomer.

The Greatest Salesman in the World - Og Mandino.

The Greatest Salesman in the World Part 2 - Og Mandino.

The 22 Immutable Laws of Branding - Al Ries.

The 11 Immutable Laws of Internet Branding - Al Ries and Laura Ries.

Positioning - The Battle for Your Mind - Al Ries and Jack Trout.

Differentiate or Die - Jack Trout.

The One Day MBA in Marketing - Michael Muckian.

Influence (Science and Practice) - Robert Cialdini.

How I Raised Myself from Failure to Success in Selling - Frank Bettger.
Secrets of Closing Sales - Roy Alexander and Charles B. Roth.
Secrets of Closing Sales - Zig Ziglar.
Selling to Win - Richard Denny.
How to Sell Anything to Anybody - Joe Girard.
It's Not How Good You Are, It's How Good You Want to Be - Paul Arden.
Advanced Selling Strategies - Brian Tracy.
The Spin Selling Fieldbook - Neil Rackham.
Increase Your Sales the Tack Way - Alfred Tack.
The Psychology of Selling - Brian Tracy.
How to Make Millions with Your Ideas - Dan Kennedy.
Being Direct - Lester Wunderman.
Closing Techniques - Stephen Schiffman.
The Power of Habits - Randy Schuster.
Guerrilla Teleselling - Jay Conrad Levinson, Mark S.A. Smith and Orvel Ray Wilson.
Secrets of Successful Telephone Selling - Robert Bly.
StreetSmart Teleselling - Jeff and Marc Slutsky.
Become a Recognised Authority in Your Field In 60 Days or Less! - Robert Bly.
Brand Yourself - David Andrusia and Rick Haskins.
Public Relations for Dummies - Eric Yaverbaum with Bob Bly.
The Origin of Brands - Al Ries and Laura Ries.
The Fall of Advertising and the Rise of PR - Al Ries and Laura Ries.
Marketing Warfare - Al Ries and Jack Trout.
Focus - Al Ries.
The 22 Immutable Laws of Marketing - Al Ries and Jack Trout.
Trout on Strategy - Jack Trout.
Selling the Invisible - Harry Beckwith.
The Power of Simplicity - Jack Trout and Steve Rivkin.
The Personal Branding Phenomenon - Peter Montoya.
Big Brands Big Trouble - Jack Trout.
Horse Sense - Al Ries and Jack Trout.
The Regis Touch - Regis McKenna.
The Copywriters Handbook - Robert Bly.
Advertising Headlines That Make You Rich - David Garfunkel.
No BS Direct Marketing - Dan Kennedy.

The Adweek Copywriting Handbook - Joseph Sugarman.
Buying Trances - Joe Vitale.
Hypnotic Writing - Joe Vitale.
The Tipping Point - Malcolm Gladwell.
Scientific Advertising - Claude Hopkins.
The Feldman Method - Andrew H. Thomson.
The Ultimate Sales Machine - Chet Holmes.
Getting Everything You Can out of All You've Got - Jay Abraham.
Commonsense Direct and Digital Marketing - Drayton Bird.
Beyond Maximarketing - Stan Rapp and Thomas L. Collins.
Magic Words That Bring You Riches - Ted Nicholas.
The Official Get Rich Guide to Information Marketing - Dan Kennedy.
Jeffrey Gitomer's Little Platinum Book of Cha-Ching! - Jeffrey Gitomer.
The Robert Collier Letter Book - Robert Collier.
A Technique for Producing Ideas - James Webb Young.
How to Sell Your Way Through Life - Napoleon Hill.
The Marketing Gurus - Chris Murray.
Stand Out! - Simon Vetter.
A New Brand World - Scott Bedbury.
How to Make Your Advertising Make Money - John Caples.
Tested Advertising Methods - John Caples.
How to Write Sales Letters That Sell - Drayton Bird.
Plug Your Book! - Steve Weber.
The New Rules of Marketing & PR - David Meerman Scott.

Personal Development / Psychological / Philosophical

Awaken the Giant Within - Anthony Robbins.
Notes from a Friend - Anthony Robbins.
Goals! - Brian Tracy.
How to Win Friends and Influence People - Dale Carnegie.
The Seven Habits of Highly Effective People - Stephen Covey.
How to Read a Book - Mortimer Adler.
The Magic of Thinking Big - David Schwartz.
As a Man Thinketh - James Allen.
Feel the Fear and Do It Anyway - Susan Jeffers.
Attracting Terrific People - Lillian Glass.
Accelerated Learning for the 21st Century - Brian Tracy and Colin Rose.

The Art of Happiness - The Dalai Lama.
The 10 Natural Laws of Successful Time and Life Management - Hyrum W. Smith.
How to Manifest Your Hearts Desire - Wayne Dyer.
The Power of Focus - Jack Canfield, Mark Victor Hansen and Les Hewitt.
Change Your Thinking Change Your Life - Brian Tracy.
The Aladdin Factor - Jack Canfield and Mark Victor Hansen.
50 Success Classics - Tom Butler-Bowden.
Live Your Dreams - Les Brown.
Life Is Tremendous - Charlie "Tremendous" Jones.
Mega Memory - Kevin Trudeau.
Dare to Win - Jack Canfield and Mark Victor Hansen.
Essential Manners for Men - Peter Post.
50 Self-Help Classics - Tom Butler-Bowdon.
WaterMelon Magic - Wally Amos & Stu Glauberman.
Tuesdays with Morrie - Mitch Albom.
Create Your Own Future - Brian Tracy.
The Success Principles - Jack Canfield.
Earl Nightingale's Greatest Discovery - Earl Nightingale.
Success Through a Positive Mental Attitude - Napoleon Hill and W. Clement Stone.
Succeed for Yourself - Richard Denny.
Chicken Soup for Your Soul - Jack Canfield and Mark Victor Hansen.
This Is Earl Nightingale - Earl Nightingale.
The 8th Habit - Stephen R. Covey.
Emotional Intelligence - Daniel Goleman.
The Work We Were Born to Do - Nick Williams.
The Book of Yo - Simon Woodroffe.
The Strangest Secret - Earl Nightingale.
Don't Sweat the Small Stuff - Richard Carlson.
Authentic - Neil Crofts.
Your Road Map for Success - John C. Maxwell.
Jonathan Livingston Seagull - Richard Bach.
The New Psycho-Cybernetics - Maxwell Maltz and Dan Kennedy.
The Dalai Lama's Book of Wisdom - The Dalai Lama.
Authentic Happiness - Martin Seligman.
Skill with People - Les Giblin.

How to Have Confidence and Power in Dealing with People - Les Giblin.
Psychology of Success - Denis Waitley.
The Secret of Creating Your Future - Tad James.
Profiles of Power and Success - Gene Landrum.
The Greatness Guide - Robin Sharma.
The Book of Questions - Gregory Stock.
The Book of Fabulous Questions - Penelope Frohart.
Positive Addiction - William Glasser.
The Law of Attraction - Ester and Jerry Hicks.
The Ultimate Gift - Jim Stovall.
The Strangest Secret - Earl Nightingale.
Lead the Field - Lesson 2 - Earl Nightingale.
Flow - Mihaly Csikszentmihalyi.
Self-Esteem - Matthew McKay & Patrick Fanning.
The Psychology of Winning - Denis Waitley.
The Midas Method - Stuart Goldsmith.
Did You Spot the Gorilla? - Richard Wiseman.
The Winners Edge - Denis Waitley.
The Magic of Believing - Claude M. Bristol.
Mental Strength - Iain Abernethy.
The Six Pillars of Self-Esteem - Nathaniel Branden.
Feeling Good - Dr David Burns.
The Pursuit of Happiness - David Myers.
Reality Therapy - William Glasser.
Choice Theory - William Glasser.
Language of Choice Theory - William Glasser.
Over the Top - Zig Ziglar.
Being the Best - Denis Waitley.
Empires of the Mind - Denis Waitley.
Self-Efficacy - Albert Bandura.
Developing Mental Toughness - Professor Graham Jones and Adrian Moorhouse.
Learned Optimism - Martin Seligman.
Motivation and Personality - Abraham Maslow.
The Survivor Personality - Al Siebert.
Bring Out the Magic in Your Mind - Al Koran.
Time Power - Brian Tracy.

Secret of the Ages - Robert Collier.
Action! - Robert Ringer.
Million Dollar Habits - Robert Ringer.
The Aptitude Test Workbook - Jim Barrett.
The Power of Your Subconscious Mind - Joseph Murphy.
Prisoners of Belief - Matthew McKay and Patrick Fanning.
The Power of Thinking Big - John C. Maxwell.
How to be Exceptional - Stuart Browne.
The Five Major Peices to the Life Puzzle - Jim Rohn.
Happy for No Reason - Marci Shimoff.
It Works - RHJ.
Adversity Quotient - Paul G. Stoltz,Phd.
Dr Robert Anthony's Advanced Formula for Total Success - Dr Robert Anthony.
The Seasons of Life - Jim Rohn.
Focal Point - Brian Tracy.
The Immune Power Personality - Henry Dreher.
Mentally Tough - Dr James E. Loehr & Peter J. McLaughlin.
On Form - Jim Loehr & Tony Schwartz.
The Corporate Athlete - Jack Groppel.
Man's Search for Meaning - Viktor E. Frankl.
Personal Power through Awareness - Sanaya Roman.
The Science of Success - Wallace D. Wattles.
The Acorn Principle - Jim Cathcart.
The Origin of Everyday Moods - Robert E. Thayer.
Stress Management for Dummies - Allen Elkin.
The Go-Giver - Bob Burg and John David Mann.
The Answer - John Assaraf and Murray Smith.
The Ten Commandments of Goal Setting - Gary Ryan Blair.
The Power of Habit - Jack Hodge.

Health

Body for Life - Bill Phillips.
Cancer - Phillip Day.
Sports Nutrition Guide - Dr Michael Colgan.
Absolution - Shawn Phillips.
The Men's Health Cover Model Workout - Owen McKibbin.

Mirror Mirror: Dr Linda's Body Image Revolution - Dr Linda Papadopoulos.
Designer Evolution - Simon Young.
Fantastic Voyage - Ray Kurzweil and Terry Grossman.
Healthy at 100 - John Robbins.
The Exercise Fix - Richard Benyo.
Psychology of Physical Activity - Stuart Biddle & Nanette Mutrie.

Spiritual / Mind Body and Spirit

Conversations with God - Neale Donald.
Living in the Light - Shakti Gawain.
The Soul of a Butterfly - Muhammad Ali and Hana Yasmeen Ali.
The Power of Now - Eckhart Tolle.
The Power of Purpose - Richard J. Leider.
The Simple Abundance Journal of Gratitude - Sarah Ban Breathnach.
The Power of Kabbalah - Yehuda Berg.
What on Earth am I Here for? - Rick Warren.
The Monk Who Sold His Ferrari - Robin S. Sharma.
The Way to Love - Anthony de Mello.
The Angel Inside - Chris Widener.
Meditation for Dummies - Stephan Bodian.
Being in Balance - Dr Wayne Dyer.
The Mastery of Love - Don Miguel Ruiz.
The Road Less Travelled - M. Scott Peck.
The Mystical Life of Jesus - Sylvia Browne.
Cosmic Consciousness - Richard Maurice Bucke.
The Ways and Power of Love - Pitirim A. Sorokin.
The Divine Matrix - Gregg Braden.

Recommended Audio

Personal Development

The Essence of Success (1-10) - Earl Nightingale.
The Psychology of Winning - Denis Waitley.
Manifest Your Destiny - Wayne Dyer.
Success Is a Journey - Brian Tracy.

The Luck Factor - Brian Tracy.
The Power of Clarity - Brian Tracy.
The Magic Word - Attitude - Earl Nightingale.
The Psychology of Achievement - Brian Tracy.
Secrets of Super Achievers - Various Speakers from Million Dollar Round Table Seminar.
Breaking the Success Barrier - Brian Tracy.
Thinking Big - Brian Tracy.
How to Talk to Anyone Anytime - Larry King.
The Science of Self-Confidence - Brian Tracy.
How to Master Your Time - Brian Tracy.
See You at the Top - Zig Ziglar.
Lead the Field - Earl Nightingale.
The 7 Habits Mastery Series - Stephen Covey.
The Art of Exceptional Living - Jim Rohn.
The Science of Personal Achievement - Napoleon Hill.
Excelling in the New Millennium - Jim Rohn Weekend Event.
The Success Principles - Jack Canfield.
The New Psycho-Cybernetics - Dr Maxwell Maltz and Dan Kennedy.
The Universal Laws of Success and Achievement - Brian Tracy.
21 Great Ways to Live to Be 100 - Brian Tracy.
Stand and Deliver - Dale Carnegie Training Company.
The Miracle of Self Discipline - Brian Tracy.
Communicate with Power - Brian Tracy.
The 80/20 Principle - Richard Koch.
The Ultimate Goals Program - Brian Tracy.
Action Strategies for Personal Achievement - Brian Tracy.
Jim Rohn Weekend Leadership Event (2004) - Jim Rohn, Brian Tracy, Denis Waitley plus others.

Wealth / Finance

Success Secrets of Self-Made Millionaires - Brian Tracy.
Multiple Streams of Income - Robert Allen.
The Road to Wealth - Robert Allen.
Think and Grow Rich - Napoleon Hill.
Million Dollar Habits - Brian Tracy.
Laws of Inner Wealth - Sir John Templeton.

The Millionaire MBA - Richard Cordock Parkes.
Your Secret Wealth - Jay Abraham.
7 Years to 7 Figures - Michael Masterson.

Sales /Marketing /Business

You're a Marketing Genius - Jay Abraham.
Mastermind Marketing Programme - Jay Abraham.
Stealth Marketing - Jay Abraham.
The Psychology of Selling - Brian Tracy.
62 Free Ways to Grow Your Business Profits - Jay Conrad Levinson.
Piranha Marketing - Joe Polish.
Magic Words That Grow Your Business - Ted Nicholas.
Advanced Selling Techniques - Brian Tracy.
Magical Marketing - Brian Tracy.
Turbo Strategy - Brian Tracy.

Investing

How to Buy Stocks - William O'Neil.
When to Sell Stocks - William O'Neil.
How to More Than Double Your Money in Mutual Funds - William O'Neil.
Beating the Street - Peter Lynch.

Business

Business Breakthroughs - Sir John Harvey Jones.
The Leader in You - Dale Carnegie.
Jim Rohn - The Weekend Seminar - Skills for the 21st Century.
The E-Myth Seminar - Michael Gerber.
The E-Myth Manager - Michael Gerber.
The Secrets of Power Negotiating - Roger Dawson.
How to Build a Network of Power Relationships - Harvey Mackay.
Leadership Mastery Course - Dale Carnegie.

APPENDIX C

Be Part of Something Different

If you have read *Liquid Millionaire* and it really grabbed you, and you want to <u>take your career to a whole new level</u>, get ready to get excited.

But before you do anything, please look at our 10 core values. These are the things that Paul and I place worth upon. These are the things that we stand for. We realise that not everybody can share our values but if you liked the book, chances are that you are going to love our values.

I sincerely hope that your values match ours because if they do, ISACO could be just what you have been looking for.

ISACO's 10 Core Values

Health

We believe that success in the areas of money, work and relationships mean absolutely nothing unless you have your health. Optimum health relates to both mind and body. It is when you are strong, flexible, pain free, independent, fit and full of energy.

Integrity

A person of integrity is one who practices and speaks the truth at all times. Integrity means you keep the promises you make—which include the promises that you make to yourself.

Financial Freedom

We believe that money allows us to have more choices in life and the more choices we have, the more control and freedom we feel. When you are financially free, money is no longer a worry. Having enough means you're able to create your ideal or dream lifestyle.

Self-improvement

For us, personal development is like a religion. We love to read books, listen to audio programs and attend seminars and classes that encourage personal growth and awareness. For us, self improvement means constant and never ending improvement in all areas of your life.

Love

We believe that it is impossible to love others more than you love yourself. And so love has to start with self. As well as loving and caring for ourselves and others, it's about loving your work and a deep and genuine love of life.

Service

We believe that you can't live a successful life unless you serve others to the best of your ability—and treat each person with the same love, respect, kindness and courtesy that you'd expect when somebody serves you.

Self-discipline

We believe that it's much easier to learn things and to talk about doing things than to actually turn your thoughts and intentions into actions. Self-discipline is therefore an essential character trait when it comes to turning your desires into reality. Self-discipline is when you do the things you know you need to do whether you feel like it or not.

Responsibility

When you are a responsible person, you don't blame, complain or finger point. You decide that the goals that are important to you are down to you and you alone. You believe that if something is going to happen, it's up to you to make it a reality.

Fun

It's important to remind ourselves on occasion not to be too serious, to lighten up, be cheerful, party, be playful, poke fun at oneself and laugh out loud.

Persistence

A person only fails if they decide to give up. But a person who persists and has the resilience to bounce back when the going gets tough is a person of courage, character and purpose. We believe that persistence is one of the most important ingredients needed in helping to turn your life into a masterpiece.

Now you have learnt about ISACO's values, here are five questions to ask yourself, to determine whether we are well suited:-

- Do you want to be part of a fabulous success story and get treated like a VIP?

- Are you hungry and ambitious and want to take your career to a whole new level?

- Do you desire to be involved in something new, unique and exciting?

- Do you want to feel like you are your own boss—and therefore experience more control over your life?

If you answered *YES!*, you may be just what we are looking for.

But let me ask you a few more questions just to make sure that we are on the same page.

- Are you known by your friends and family to be positive, hardworking and enthusiastic?

- As well as a values match, do you like our mission and credo? - Are they also in alignment with yours?

- Are you a people person? Do people tell you that you are warm and friendly?

- Do you have a genuine interest in personal and professional development?

- Do you love to read books that can help you grow, listen to audio programs to help you learn new skills and attend seminars to give you even more awareness?

- Are you known as a go-getter, a person who never gives up, and are prepared to do whatever it takes to ensure you get to your goals?

- Do you love the way we think and want to be part of the process of helping clients to retire liquid rich?

If you are still with me, you might be pleased to hear that if you are accepted, before you know it, you could be earning a six figure income.

We will also do everything in our power to ensure you retire liquid rich—so that you can live and experience your very own dream lifestyle.

You will receive excellent training and we would continually encourage and support you in reaching your true potential.

If you want to be part of a fast growing dynamic company with huge goals, email us NOW at <u>Support@ISACO.co.uk</u> with the words **"I'm Interested in Joining Your Winning Team."**

If you haven't already, take a look at our mission and credo. That way you can really determine whether we are singing from the same hymn sheet. If there is a match, get excited!

ISACO's Mission and Credo

ISACO's Mission

Our Mission as a Company:

To Become the Most Admired and Respected ISA Trend Investing Support Company in the UK.

Our Mission to You:

To Help Make Your Financial Dreams Reality.

ISACO's Credo

People First

At ISACO it's all about relationships. If we focus on helping all of our stakeholders achieve their goals, the company will achieve its goals at the same time. People first, products second, profits third.

Products Second

Create the best products and services to help our clients reach their goal of retiring liquid rich.

Profits Third

If our focus is on people first and products and services second, then profits will inevitably follow.

So, as I just mentioned, if you want to be part of a fast growing, dynamic company with huge goals, email us NOW at Support@ISACO.co.uk with the words **"I'm Interested in Joining Your Winning Team."**

Good Luck!

Your friend,

Stephen

PS. As I said before, I sincerely hope that your values match ours because if they do, ISACO could be just what you've been looking for.

DISCLAIMER

We endeavour to deliver quality information, ideas and personal opinions on stocks, funds and the general market. However, the information, ideas and personal opinions provided are intended to be a general guide to financial management only.

This book is intended to be a guide to financial management. Stephen Sutherland, ISACO Ltd and its employees are not agents, brokers, stockbrokers, broker dealers or registered financial advisors. The author does not accept any responsibility for loss occasioned to any person acting or refraining from acting as a result of material contained in this book.

Stephen Sutherland and ISACO Ltd do not recommend particular stocks or investment funds or any other security or any other investment of any kind. If particular stocks or investment funds are mentioned, they are mentioned only for illustrative and educational purposes.

Whilst Stephen Sutherland and ISACO Ltd comment on the services and advice offered by other companies and individuals, none of these owners have authorised, sponsored, endorsed or approved this publication.

Stephen Sutherland or ISACO Ltd have not received any remuneration in return for including any company or product in this book.

It is recommended that you seek advice from a registered financial professional prior to implementing any investment program or financial plan.

Stephen Sutherland and ISACO Ltd, their agent and employees, do not guarantee any results or investment returns based on the information in this program.

Past performance is no indication or guarantee of future results and the value of any investment you make can go down as well as up. This book presents information and opinions believed to be reliable, but the accuracy cannot be guaranteed. Stephen Sutherland and ISACO Ltd are not responsible for any errors or omissions.

INDEX

Symbols

7% withdrawal formula 19, 23
  examples 24, 57, 59, 157, 161

A

adviser, becoming one's own li, 82
age rejuvenation therapy 162
Akami Technologies 13
Allen, Robert xviii, lii, 5, 221, 222, 230
Ameritrade (brokerage company) xxi, 7,
  10, 188
Apple Inc 13
Applied Materials 142
Archimedes 15
ASM (Automatic Success Mechanism)
  21
Aurelius, Marcus 22
Awaken the Giant Within (Robbins)
  225
AXA Framlington Japan Fund 41, 46,
  97, 98, 186

B

Baidu.com Inc 13
Bandura, Albert xix, 4, 179, 227
Baruch, Bernard xvii, 145, 219
bear markets 220
  duration of 35, 60, 62, 63
  Nasdaq xxviii, xxxi, xxxii, xlv, li, 9, 46,
    51, 82, 89, 95, 96, 97, 98, 99, 100,
    101, 103, 104, 109, 110, 113,
    116, 132, 141, 142, 145, 146,
    172, 185, 186, 187, 188, 190,
    191, 192, 196, 197, 201
  rallies 8
  reading the market xxxi, 136, 140,
    142, 144

recommended advice 239
  switching 42, 57, 120, 124, 139, 146,
    150
belief, power of 55, 157, 159, 160
  self-belief 179
Blair, Gary Ryan 23, 228
Branson, Richard xviii, 61, 219
Brin, Serge 176
Bristol, Claude M. xix, 160, 227
Buddha 22
Buffet, Warren 33, 110
bull markets (uptrends) 83, 84
  and strengths 3
  duration of 35, 60, 62, 63
  predicting end of 146
  purchase of funds, timing 1
  reading the market xxxi, 136, 140,
    142, 144
  recommended advice 239
  start of xxxvii, 3, 6, 91, 189
buy and hold strategy 42, 133

C

CAN SLIM™ 8
Carlson, Richard xviii, xix, 49, 222, 226
case studies 57, 58, 59, 65, 77
Cash ISAs l, 81
cause and effect, universal law of 155
charts, using xxvii, li, 81, 93, 136, 140,
  148, 150
  Nasdaq xxvii, li, 81, 93, 136, 140, 148,
    150
  QQQQ (exchange-traded fund) 141
chips (semiconductors) 27, 141, 142
choice, power of 155
Churchill, Winston 184
Cisco Systems 141
clarity 230

V

W

Printed in the United Kingdom by
Lightning Source UK Ltd., Milton Keynes
138311UK00003B/2/P